# TOWARDS BULLY-FREE SCHOOLS

# TOWARDS BULLY-FREE SCHOOLS

**Derek Glover** and **Netta Cartwright**
with **Denis Gleeson**

OPEN UNIVERSITY PRESS
Buckingham · Philadelphia

Open University Press
Celtic Court
22 Ballmoor
Buckingham
MK18 1XW

and
1900 Frost Road, Suite 101
Bristol, PA 19007, USA

First Published 1998

A catalogue record of this book is available from the British Library

ISBN   0 335 19929 1 (pb)   0 335 19930 5 (hb)

*Library of Congress Cataloging-in-Publication Data*
Glover, Derek.
    Anti-bullying in action / Derek Glover and Netta Cartwright with Denis
Gleeson.
        p.   cm.
    Includes bibliographical references and index.
    ISBN 0-335-19930-5  (hardcover). —  ISBN 0-335-19929-1  (pbk.)
    1. School violence—Great Britain—Prevention—Case studies.
    2. Bullying—Great Britain—Prevention—Case studies.  I. Cartwright, Netta.
    II. Gleeson, Denis.  III. Title.
LB3013.3.G58   1998
371.7′82—dc21                                                                        97-23200
                                                                                          CIP

Typeset by Type Study, Scarborough
Printed in Great Britain by Biddles Ltd, Guildford and King's Lynn

# CONTENTS

# PREFACE

Awareness of the adverse effects of bullying within schools has increased in the past ten years – it is no longer accepted as a necessary part of the school experience. The response within schools has been varied but most schools now consider the issues seriously and have developed either specific policies or general policies of which the management of anti-social behaviour is a part.

This book is based upon research by the Department of Education at Keele University within the schools which hosted associate teachers during their year of training for the Postgraduate Certificate in Education – known locally as 'the Partnership'. The methodology was a combination of questionnaire survey conducted by the staff of the Department, interviews with pupils undertaken by the associate teachers after training, interviews with staff undertaken by the staff from Keele and a wide-ranging documentary search. The research team acknowledges with gratitude the willing help from the schools and their pupils who showed no reticence in sharing their thoughts. Without their openness and, we believe, honesty, the investigation would have been a statistical exercise rather than an opportunity to share in what it means to be a pupil at school in the 1990s. The inspiration of Dr Mervyn Taylor, formerly Head of Department at Keele, was fundamental to the project both as a partnership activity and as a research exercise aimed at improving the school life of many pupils.

The materials provided by the schools have been considered alongside the data which give some indication of the effectiveness of policies and programmes in changing perceptions and practice within and beyond school communities. In Chapter 1 we link the research context and the reality of school life. Chapter 2 is based upon the experiences of a group of young people and leads to a consideration of the impact of anti-bullying within the project schools in Chapter 3. The central contention of the research is that policies are only of limited value unless they are part of a positive overall culture of the school and this is considered in Chapter 4 before looking at the way in which policies have evolved and the detail and help which they give in Chapter 5. We also contend that much change has to come from outside the school and Chapters 6 and 7 are concerned with the role of parents and the community in achieving changed attitudes. The process of change in the schools which have been successful in implementing anti-bullying policies is explored in Chapter 8 and the reality of change is shown in the three case studies outlined in Chapter 9. Chapter 10 concludes by revisiting the approach to developing positive school culture as the key to effective anti-bullying strategies.

In the expectation that many readers will be concerned with the development of policy and the changing of attitudes within their own schools we have added occasional 'Reflection' points to the text in all except the final chapter in the hope that they will encourage discussion. We have also given examples of the materials being developed within the schools in the project but much more detail of both the research data and the materials is given in the report to the Partnership available from the Department of Education at Keele University.

Mention is made of the practice in the schools but we have used pseudonyms to avoid any false interpretation based upon incomplete data. However, there is much to be gained from some knowledge of the background of the schools and the table on page x summarizes the main features of the sample schools.

As authors, we are presenting the findings of a team of people who have worked together over the year of the project. Professor Denis Gleeson has been both mentor and reviewer as we have progressed with this book; Michael Johnson has collected and collated all the open comment which formed such an important part of the evidence of what the pupils really thought and Gerry Gough has analysed the considerable statistical data from the questionnaire to point to our conclusions and to identify those aspects which require further investigation. Nothing would have been possible without the willing help and readiness to review issues in the Partnership schools – we count our involvement with them as a great privilege. We also acknowledge the unstinting secretarial support given to the project by Gladys Pye. The work continues with David Miller, as Director of the PGCE course, and with Michael Boulton as consultant, as we understand more of the relationships between personal and contextual factors in the development of pupil attitudes. Above all, however, we are seeking yet more evidence that intervention does make a lasting difference.

Derek Glover, Keele Partnership Project Coordinator 1997
Netta Cartwright, Teacher Fellow, Keele Partnership, 1997

# ABOUT THE AUTHORS

*Derek Glover* was for 18 years head of Burford School and Community College in Oxfordshire. He moved into higher education in 1990 and completed his PhD in community perceptions of school effectiveness working with the Open University. During this period he worked with the University of Leicester on the earliest grant-maintained schools. As a research fellow with the University of Keele he has worked on a number of projects including the evaluation of PGCE courses, aspects of vocational training, and mentoring initial teacher education, and continuing professional development. He currently teaches financial management on the MA and MBA courses at Keele and has been associated with the Open University in research into financial effectiveness in schools. Publications include *Managing Autonomous Schools* (with Tony Bush and Marianne Coleman; Paul Chapman, 1993), *The Management of Mentoring* (with George Mardle; Kogan Page, 1995) and *Managing Professional Development in Education* (with Sue Law; Kogan Page, 1996).

*Netta Cartwright*, a graduate of Aberystwyth, Cardiff and Keele Universities, has taught in primary, middle and secondary schools and worked as a TVEI Evaluator and an Adviser on Equal Opportunities. She is the School Counsellor and Coordinator of Equal Opportunities and Anti-Bullying work at Walton High School, Stafford as well as teaching English. Since 1984 she has initiated and developed equal opportunities, peer-counselling and anti-bullying strategies at this and other Staffordshire schools. She has published 'Guidelines for Action Towards Equal Opportunities (Gender)' and several articles and chapters on using counselling to tackle bullying and sexual harassment. These include: *Journal for a Just and Caring Education* (Sage Publications, USA); *Peer Counselling Networker* (Roehampton Institute, London); *Counselling in Education Newsletter* (British Association for Counselling, UK); *Present Time* (Rational Island Publishers, USA); and *Peer Counselling in Schools* (David Fulton Publishers, London).

*Denis Gleeson* is Professor and Head of the Department of Education at Keele University. He is also the Director of the Centre for Post-Compulsory Education and Training (CPET) and Director of Research. In recent years he has been involved in a number of major research projects looking at youth, school, further education and employment issues. He is presently involved in two research projects: an ESRC project researching Changing Teaching and Managerial Cultures in FE, and a study of Middle Management in Schools funded by the Central England Training and Enterprise Council. He has published extensively and his most recent book, *Knowledge and Nationhood: Education, politics and work*, was published by Cassell in 1996.

# SUMMARY OF SCHOOLS

To avoid any intrusion we have used pseudonyms throughout but the detail of the 25 schools taking part is as follows.

| School | Control* | Age range | Roll | Catchment | Questionnaire responses† |
|---|---|---|---|---|---|
| Boundary | LEA | 11–16 | 800 | Urban | 157 |
| Canalside | LEA | 11–18 | 1100 | Rural | 179 |
| Cathedral | LEA | 11–16 | 900 | Urban | 172 |
| Downlands | LEA | 11–16 | 1000 | Urban | 113 |
| Far Edge | LEA | 11–18 | 900 | Urban | 168 |
| Forest Bank | LEA | 11–18 | 572 | Urban | 134 |
| Greendale | LEA | 11–18 | 1300 | Mixed | 248 |
| Greensward | LEA | 11–18 | 900 | Mixed | 204 |
| Greylands | LEA | 11–18 | 800 | Urban | 176 |
| Heathlands | LEA | 11–18 | 1100 | Rural | 207 |
| High Bank | LEA | 13–18 | 800 | Rural | 171 |
| Highlands | LEA | 11–16 | 900 | Urban | 166 |
| Longmeadow | LEA | 11–18 | 1000 | Urban | 114 |
| Lowlands | LEA | 11–18 | 1050 | Mixed | 209 |
| Northings | LEA | 11–18 | 1000 | Mixed | 204 |
| Oakley | LEA | 11–16 | 800 | Mixed | 146 |
| Parklands | LEA | 11–16 | 700 | Urban | 191 |
| Reedwood | LEA | 11–16 | 1200 | Urban | 185 |
| Rivermead | LEA | 11–18 | 1400 | Mixed | 211 |
| Springlands | GM | 11–18 | 700 | Urban | 196 |
| Towers | LEA | 11–16 | 900 | Mixed | 141 |
| Townend | LEA | 11–18 | 1300 | Urban | 225 |
| Wallsend | GM | 11–18 | 900 | Mixed | 197 |
| Westwards | LEA | 13–18 | 600 | Mixed | 204 |
| Wysdom | LEA | 13–18 | 900 | Rural | 172 |

* LEA = local education authority; GM = grant-maintained.
† Total of 4490.

# ① FEELINGS OF SECURITY

## Introduction

During the second half of the 1980s, the educational scene was dominated by the Education Reform Act 1988. Public political concern with the detail of this legislation, however, inhibited widespread consideration of the proposals in the report of the committee investigating Discipline in Schools, chaired by Lord Elton (DES 1989). This report suggested that disruption affecting teaching and learning was caused by cumulative minor misbehaviour rather than by single isolated incidents of indiscipline. In order to develop policies to counter such problems, the committee suggested that schools should become more concerned with the establishment of a sense of shared values and with a collective responsibility amongst all staff for the culture of the school. Unfortunately, because of the apparently more pressing issues of local management of schools, pupil recruitment, grant-maintained status and the National Curriculum emerging from the implementation of the 1988 Act, the Elton report was paid only limited attention in many schools.

At government level there was a view that schools had to be forced to consider the ways in which they could become more effective. Work which had begun with Rutter *et al.* (1979) in an investigation of the effectiveness of secondary schools and then been extended to the primary field by Mortimore *et al.* (1988) had highlighted the need for raised expectations by staff, pupils and parents, as a prerequisite for the attainment of higher standards of achievement. Alongside this work the development of the pastoral curriculum (Galloway 1985) was becoming recognized as an essential for the delivery of cross-curricular themes, and for the promotion of positive interpupil attitudes. The debate on the content of the National Curriculum focused on improvement through consistent and assessed practice in a system where schools were being competitively set against each other as outlined by Bowe and Ball (1992).

The policymakers in schools realized that in this market situation there was a link between discipline and public perceptions of the school which in turn affected the ability of a school to recruit to capacity and thus ensure continuing levels of funding. Good discipline was seen as one of the hallmarks of good schools, as illustrated amongst others by the Scottish Education Department (1989), Hunter (1991) and Glover (1992). A significant element in discipline management, already identified by the Elton report, was control of bullying. This was reported as a widespread problem with damaging effects on the individual pupil and on school atmosphere. This assertion was given further weight with the widespread media attention to the prevalence of bullying following the publication of research in the UK based upon earlier work undertaken in Scandinavia (Olweus 1978). From the UK research, Tattum and Lane (1989) and Besag (1989), identified the incidence and effects of bullying on the school experience of pupils of all ages and backgrounds. The media attention through television programmes such as *That's Life* led to the production of packs of materials which could be used by those schools which were prepared to recognize that there might be a problem and that intervention could be beneficial. These packs were produced through government action, for example *Bullying: don't suffer in silence* (DfE 1994), or through charity aid, for example, The Gulbenkian Foundation (Besag 1992).

The effect of parental and public interest has been to develop anti-bullying policies within schools. The impact of these has been outlined either as particular tactics have been introduced (Boulton and Flemington 1996), or as strategies have been variously applied across a group of schools (Smith and Sharp 1994). Whilst much of the research material has been produced very recently, it is based upon interventions which have been under consideration within schools since 1989. The Keele Partnership of schools, primarily associated to facilitate initial teacher education, decided in 1995 to investigate the continuing impact of anti-bullying policies in schools. The group had been prompted to carry out the investigation because of the evidence mounting from parent and pupil attitude surveys being undertaken as part of a school self-evaluation process used by schools across the country. Fifteen per cent of the 7500 parents responding by June 1995 believed that their children were sometimes bullied and 18 per cent believed that bullying was a problem in the schools their children attended. The evidence also showed that children from groups facing financial hardship were proportionately more likely to suffer from bullying by others (Glover *et al.* 1997). The Keele Partnership planning group felt that if these statistics were to be substantiated as a result of more detailed investigation, it would indicate that current anti-bullying interventions were only having limited effect.

All schools in the Keele Partnership were invited to take part in an investigation which would provide reports confidential to each school, as well as general data based upon the aggregate of results. It was agreed that the emphasis should be on peer relationships and social life in and out of school and that the term 'bullying' would not be used as any part of the focus in materials and interview schedules. Whether because of the terminology used by staff within schools, or simply because the issue was seen as fundamental to all relationships, it was apparent that pupils considered that they were taking part in an investigation into bullying behaviour. Pupils were consequently open in what they said but at the same time staff within the schools have commented that these comments may place too much emphasis on what they believe to be a minor problem. The view of the research team was that the questionnaire responses would indicate the extent of the problem by uncovering some of the detail of self-confessed behaviour.

---

**Reflection**    'Problems for a few are being made too much of.' What are the research problems inherent in an investigation where this is a frequently expressed attitude?

---

Twenty-five schools agreed to participate and to allow one-quarter of their pupils to complete the survey questionnaire, yielding 4700 completed responses. All these respondents were invited to make anonymous open comments on any aspects of peer relationships and school life. The schools also agreed that up to 10 pupils from across the age groups in each school would be interviewed following a structured format. These interviews were conducted by student teachers, known as 'associates', following a training day held at the university. A cross-section of staff were then interviewed by the education tutors working with each school so that policies could be set within their context and the detail of intervention teased out. Full sets of data were developed for 13 schools, partial interview data was obtained from a further seven, and questionnaire responses only from a further five schools.

## Themes

Attention had been paid to previous work in determining the themes for the partnership investigation. The concept of 'bullying' was clearly open to multiple interpretation amongst the staff of the schools, ranging from 'any act by one member of the group which caused annoyance or distress to any other member of the group', to 'physical hurt'. In order to clarify the issue, particularly where pupils were to be asked to reflect on their experiences, the elements of Olweus' (1989, 1993) definition were considered to be fundamental to the interpretation of the term for questionnaire analysis purposes. These elements are:

- *exposure over time or repeatedly*, which was intended to overcome the 'once off' altercation;
- *negative actions*, which included any elements of physical, verbal or social hurt; and
- *one or more students*, reflecting the variety of individual or group actions.

Given that the age group under investigation was 11–16 years, the team decided that the exploration of patterns of social behaviour would be probed in the interviews.

The advantage of using the Olweus definition was that subsequent work by other investigators had used his approach and by following a similar concept of bullying any data could be used for statistical comparison. The earliest large-scale research undertaken by Olweus in Norway in 1983 with a group of 130 000 pupils aged 8 to 16 years, had shown 9 per cent of the group as victims, 7 per cent as bullies and 1.6 per cent as both bully and victim. The frequency of these actions was described as 'now and then or more frequently'. For the Keele Partnership work we settled on a definition of 'in the past school year' but then modified this to allow for an estimate of frequency within this parameter. Mooij (1993) reporting on an investigation in 1991 with 1055 secondary pupils found a more open level of admission with 16 per cent believing that they had bullied, and only 6 per cent considering themselves to be the victims. The Sheffield investigation (Ahmad *et al.* 1991) working with 4135 secondary pupils at the end of 1990, established that 6 per cent thought that they had indulged in bullying whilst 4 per cent thought that they suffered as victims once a week or more frequently, and 10 per cent thought that they were victimized sometimes or more frequently. Although definitions and questionnaires varied, it seemed that some 20 per cent of pupils in all surveys were either bullies or victims to a greater or lesser extent. Research in the USA based on a 1993 survey of 6504 high-school students failed to ask respondents to state whether they bullied but 12 per cent were regularly victims, 25 per cent thought that they were at risk of being or becoming victims and 56 per cent said that they had witnessed victimization within their schools. The problem is both significant and widespread.

This work established a benchmark for the Keele Partnership investigation – seeking to see whether, within comparable data, there had been an improvement as a result of intervention within the schools. The Sheffield project was extended after 1991 with closely monitored and recorded intervention in each of the schools giving a set of comparators on the effect of changing school policies (Smith and Sharp 1994). The earlier investigations had also considered in varying degrees the race, gender, ability and social context of bullying behaviours. In brief, these were a tendency for boys to be more aggressive and 'physical' in their bullying (Siann 1994), for bullying to decline with age (Whitney and Smith 1993) and for bullying to be more marked in socially and culturally disadvantaged areas (Cutright 1995). Part of the purpose of the Keele Partnership investigation was to ascertain whether anti-bullying measures in schools had had any effect on predispositions for particular behaviour patterns. Understanding of who the bullies and the victims were, and how they acted both as individuals and socially, was considered to be fundamental in establishing more effective policies.

These considerations led to further consideration of Olweus's (1993) classification of the major group of victims as 'passive or submissive' and who accept teasing, physical hurt, extortion or social exclusion without any retaliation except at the point of losing control. A smaller group, his 'proactive' victims are the students who provoke others to bully them by hyperactivity, social deviance or, in the words of one of our interviewees 'being somebody who simply asks for it'. Typical bullies are seen by Olweus to offer a combination of aggression and physical strength, although Neary and Joseph (1994) has shown that the latter element is not necessarily present in girls. The readiness to be part of a group reinforcing leadership by a strong bully may lead students to become 'passive bullies' who would not act unless they were spurred on to do so. Such a classification is complicated by the existence of students who will be the victim in one relationship but then become the bully in another and the Keele Partnership investigation was concerned to establish the patterns which operated between gender, age, ability and social group membership for the 'bully/victims'. Schwartz (1993) offers a classification which defines these as 'aggressive victims' compared with 'aggressive non-victims', the traditional bullies. He also sees those who are neither victim nor bullied as 'normative contrasts' who may, however, set the parameters which define bullying behaviour. Clearly, the Keele Partnership investigation needed to follow these classifications to see how far staff in schools were recognizing the behaviour patterns and developing applicable strategies for coping with individual needs.

The efforts made by the staff of schools to overcome bullying and to establish an atmosphere conducive to positive relationships as a basis for effective teaching and learning were described as 'interventions'. The Keele Partnership study aimed at establishing the context within which schools were developing these interventions. The information for this was elicited from the questionnaire responses and from interview evidence. The degree of match between perceived policies, 'what the teachers think happens', and the reality as understood by students, 'what goes on', was considered to be a further measure of the effectiveness of anti-bullying policies. Consideration of successful policies as outlined by previous researchers led to the use of a classification of action. The most immediate group of interventions are associated with *crisis* management when student–student relationships break down. These include coping with the situation in a way which avoids worsening relationships, discussion of actions and counselling and planning for longer term individual support, as outlined by Pearce (1991) and Mellor (1991). Intervention to open up opportunities for students to discuss and understand behaviour, both action and reaction, can be fostered through *curriculum* development. This may be as a discrete component of personal, social and health education, or as part of the English, drama, history or RE syllabus as outlined by Cowie and Sharp (1994) and Tattum and Herbert (1993). Much less specific are interventions which are intended to affect the *culture* of the school. This includes the establishment of a set of values which are understood by both staff and students as the norm for the school, the empowerment of pupils so that they can manage relationships at their own level, and the development of known, consistent and positive actions to foster positive relationships. This group of interventions is described by Tattum and Herbert as 'management strategies' but Olweus (1991) uses the phrase 'school climate'. The Sheffield project (Higgins 1994) interpreted the culture of the school to include the physical environment as a reflection of the care and consideration made possible through minimizing opportunities for anti-social behaviour in corners of the school which were not regularly seen by staff, and through the development of positive activities within the leisure areas. The Keele Partnership research aimed to find out how far school climate, interpreted in its widest sense, was being changed in order to meet anti-bullying needs and whether crisis, curriculum or cultural interventions on their own were making a difference to student experience. Whether, in fact, the existence of known crisis intervention could act as a sufficient deterrent to further bullying, whether curriculum topics were fostering more positive attitudes, and whether the reality matched the rhetoric of cultural change.

## Context

The schools in the project are all either local education authority (LEA) or grant-maintained (GM) schools. They serve communities ranging from the inner urban (eight schools) to those on the urban–suburban fringe (eleven schools), and those drawing upon predominantly suburban and rural areas (six schools). This gives evidence from students drawn from all social classes and provides interview data on the effect of the environment on student attitudes especially with regard to social mores and acceptable behaviour in and out of school. The effect of anti-bullying policies would be limited if there was evidence of a clash between the culture of the school and the culture of the larger community. This issue has been particularly followed by the Home Office (1995) working upon the organizational culture of the school in its environment. This leads to consideration of the socio-economic context of the home. The Keele schools included two with over 60 per cent of students having free school meals, and two with less than 5 per cent doing so and, whilst this does not necessarily relate to the nature and degree of parental support, Table 1.1 does show a tendency for parents who believe that they are comfortably off to think that their children are not being bullied whilst those from disadvantaged backgrounds appear to be bullied more frequently. The data for this table are derived from the national surveys of 7500 parents undertaken by the Centre for Successful Schools at Keele and indicate the need for further investigation of the nature of home support of both bullies and victims. Compton and Baizerman (1991) have demonstrated how low resourcing for counselling and support of students in this situation is exacerbated by the adverse conditions of the home environment and may promote a readiness to act aggressively but Rutherford and Billig (1995) have shown how the development of parental advocacy can help overcome the tendency for the disadvantaged to accept rather than counter their situation as a victim.

Much depends upon the culture of the home irrespective of the socio-economic context. Where retaliation is the expected norm tensions develop between home and school and Marano (1995) suggests that school and home need to have the same view of self-discipline, self-control and self-esteem rather than aggression in handling relationships. Where the home view is that the school is too soft in its attitude any tendency to aggressive behaviour appears to be upheld by the parents as an assertion of self-defence, where the school is considered to be too hard, recalcitrant students feel that they are supported by parents defending them when they are 'picked on'. The success of anti-bullying strategies is inhibited where students can utilise these tensions – a reflection of the research undertaken by Stanley (1995) who investigated computer hacking, raving and joy-riding as acceptable to many parents and 'nothing to do with the school'.

**Table 1.1** Parental opinion of frequency of bullying according to family circumstances

|  | No difficulty (%) | Tending to no difficulty (%) | Tending (%) | In difficulty (%) | Total (%) |
|---|---|---|---|---|---|
| Not at all | 74 | 67 | 63 | 56 | 69 |
| Rarely | 14 | 16 | 15 | 15 | 15 |
| Sometimes | 10 | 14 | 18 | 25 | 14 |
| Regularly | 2 | 2 | 3 | 4 | 2 |

> **Reflection**   Is there a difference between the acceptability of hacking and bullying as behaviours? How can this be considered within the moral and spiritual framework of the curriculum?

## Focus

The student may feel that he or she is defended by, or detached from, the community and home context but has to live within the school and develop as an individual. This leads to consideration of the growth of self-esteem based on the concept that those who are lacking in social confidence and competence, are more likely to bully and to be bullied than those who feel at ease with their environment. Olweus (1993) relates propensity to bully to physical superiority, and the potential for victimization to those who are external deviants, different in appearance, competence or physical strength from the normative group of that age or ability. But bullying is now accepted as having much more complex origins and manifestations. Tattum *et al.* (1993) classify bullying behaviours as physical, verbal, gesture, extortion and exclusion behaviours. These activities do not require the physical superiority mentioned by Olweus – they require the ability to instil fear and the power to impose a strong will over others. With the widening of perceptions of bullying, the success of anti-bullying policies requires action on a broad front so that all students are helped to feel valued.

Where anti-bullying policies have been developed and implemented, positive relationships will offer feelings of security. These are again complex – the student is developing physically, mentally and socially through adolescence, reflecting the nature of upbringing and the culture of the community and home, and reacting to each new situation. The components of security were used as the basis of the Keele Partnership questionnaires with a structure based upon:

- Self – race, gender, age, physical and academic ability or disability, self-image.
- School – size, type, organization, pastoral support, culture.
- Home – affluence, values, culture, attitudes.
- Community – values, cohesion, tensions, resources.

The interrelationships between these various factors are complex in the extreme and the way in which the change in one variant can affect development overall has been pursued by Lister (1995) in tracing the impact of a 'fresh start' geographical move on one family – the son could not be considered in isolation from the social group. Mooij (1993) offers a similar classification but distinguishes between the following:

- Personal characteristics – personality traits.
- Early home socialization characteristics – parental aggressiveness, punishment, and norms.
- Social processes – affective, cooperative, disruptive and power characteristics of relationships.
- School characteristics – organization, opportunity, culture.
- Societal characteristics – status orientation, dominance and power.

This classification contains all the elements of the questionnaire but is rather more dynamic and less descriptive. In an attempt to look at the way in which interaction and the mechanics of relationships condition the student experience, there was more emphasis on discussion of process in analysing narratives offered by pupils in the interviews.

Anti-bullying policies are effective in the school at the time when they are actively pursued. The comment from one of the interviewees, expressing sentiments evident in three different schools, that

> they need to remind us frequently that we have signed anti-bullying contracts rather than hoping that by signing we will remember what we said then

suggests that the pressure of life in schools is such that the focus of staff attention slips until crisis intervention is needed and then the whole-school policy is reinvigorated. As a result, few pupils can objectively assess the impact of developmental change – the investigation was therefore concerned with the pupil perception of the extant school culture rather than with longitudinal change. However, by interviewing students from all age groups, it was possible to gain an impression of the way things are now compared with earlier experience of life in the school. Much of the open comment provided evidence of the emphasis which students felt was being placed on anti-bullying policies at the time.

The feelings of security thus became the basis of the investigation and the purpose of policy development was seen to be an enhancement of this feature of school life. The way in which each school in the cohort develops policies, action plans and monitoring and evaluation appears fundamental to student perception of the way in which they are protected. For this reason, the investigation has concentrated not only on the student experience but also on the way in which the school develops both the philosophy and the practice of student care. The material obtained from the staff interviews offers a background to the questionnaire and interview data for each school and shows the importance of staff attitudes. In one school, a senior member of staff commented that

> there is value in learning to live with a degree of intimidation for all students

and yet, on paper at least, a thorough student support system exists with encouragement for students to disclose details of anti-social behaviour. Part of the focus of the investigation was, therefore, to establish the way in which staff foster or inhibit the organizational and philosophical basis of anti-bullying policy.

The purposes of the investigation have therefore been to establish the following:

- The extent of bullying within the sample schools.
- To determine whether this has been affected by the development of anti-bullying policies and practices.
- To relate student perceptions to the contextual situation of home, school and community.
- To ascertain the extent to which the above three elements are inter-related in establishing feelings of security.

The questionnaire investigated these issues through the following:

- Establishing personal data including self-image and self-concept indicators.
- Asking for student experience of a variety of anti-social activities both as participant and victim.
- Seeking the motivation which leads to anti-social behaviour directed against others.
- Establishing the response to anti-social behaviour by the student, his or her peers and the staff.
- Determining students' feelings about security within school.
- Asking the student to assess his or her relationships with home and community.

These data, together with the notes of all interviews and the documentary evidence gathered from all participating schools, provide the material for consideration of the issues raised in this chapter. Whilst the school-specific analysis of material is confidential to each school, general discussion does investigate the relationship between the incidence and impact of anti-bullying policies and the context of schools but without disclosing actual names. The focus of our attention has been on the effect and permanence of change achieved by developing and implementing policies in schools, and we explore this further in the case studies of school policy in action. However, the starting point is less institutional and more individual and we have used evidence from face-to-face interviews to illustrate personal experience and the interpretation placed upon this by pupils.

# 2  ME – COMING TO TERMS WITH SELF-IMAGE

## Introduction

Chapter 1 has outlined the rationale and process of the research into understanding the way in which young people behave. In this chapter, we outline the experience and reflection on that experience by eight students of differing age, ability and personality. Their evidence provides an insight into adolescent feelings during a period when personality is maturing and attitudes are being formed. Two admit to bullying others, two feel that they are victims, two fit into the bully/victim category and two offer the views of those who watch from the sidelines. The intention is not to offer the horror stories of research, but rather to show how bullying is variously interpreted, explained and managed by the students and how they feel that school policies could support them more effectively. The discussion also illustrates the way in which each student has a view of his or her own self-image and how this fits within the concepts of personal security.

## Case studies

### The primary-to-secondary school transition

Discussion with this girl, Katherine, showed how the transition from primary to secondary school can create difficulties for those who have problems in adjusting to new environments. Katherine was also aware that she did not fit the pattern which the more sophisticated urban girls had established in the new organization. However, clear induction, communication of firm action in the event of problems, and confidence in key staff helped her to overcome her feelings as a victim during the settling-in year.

*Katherine – Year 7*

Katherine was a bright, open and fairly confident Year 7 girl in a large town comprehensive school but lived at some distance in a close village community. She showed some elements of a behaviour which she described as 'being a goody two shoes' and resented the views that others had that it was 'cool to be tough'. At the same time she was aware that she was being criticized by others because she was unable to have 'bags or shoes which are hip enough' for mainstream acceptance. To her there is a sequence of aggressive behaviour initially by one, but then by a group, which results 'in unhappiness, feeling all alone, making you sad, and then convincing you that nobody likes you'. She was aware that others can judge unhappiness and that it is necessary to preserve an outward appearance of being tough if people ask what is wrong. It was also important to avoid reporting any incidents to staff although the emphasis in assemblies and tutorial work in her school was on the need to tell a member of staff in the event of personal unhappiness. Katherine was however, somewhat confused in thinking about this because she spoke of a year head in whom she had complete confidence and to whom it is possible to speak without things getting out of hand, and then mentioned other staff who would give support but would then let the bully know about any complaint and she was fearful of consequent recrimination. Parents and older siblings were able to 'stick up for you' at this stage and she was aware that this could get bullies into really deep trouble so that they would be scared to try anything in the future.

Katherine considered that the school had a good system but that much depended upon the relationship of students and staff. An element of immaturity emerged in her view that 'some people want to get into trouble because they want to be tough like that and for others this becomes a put on, but it's really bad that this happens and people should behave but then others turn on you if you dob on them'. She felt that the bully is a person who exerts power over others to act against those who are different in some way. Relationships with parents are important because they provide the support against other people and the school is prepared to listen to them but Katherine spoke of a problem where parents 'are not prepared to believe that their children can be in the wrong'. To her, the fundamental requirement was that she should be counted as one of the group and that staff should compensate for the problems emerging from the size of the secondary school.

### The pecking order

This is a reflection of an attempt to gain a place in the pecking order when students change from primary to secondary school and illustrates the way in which a young boy, Chris, who admits to minor bullying, perceives school policies. It also shows how being able to stand up against others is seen as an essential prerequisite for 'feeling good'. He admitted to 'falling out' with others but believed that this does not constitute bullying.

*Chris – Year 8*

Chris was a lively, middle-ability boy in Year 8 of a small comprehensive school. He moved into the school with a group of friends from primary school and considered that he was a popular member of the class. He was physically mature for his age and showed an ambivalent attitude to bullying. Although he has sometimes fallen out with others and this has resulted in fights both in and out of school, he argued that this is not bullying but arises because people get carried away in playing together and that he has to defend himself. This usually led to a feeling of frustration because he had been 'involved in a fight which he never really wanted on his part' and he regretted that he inevitably lost friends as a result of his actions. At the same time, he found it difficult to accept that he might have been to blame and always saw fault to lie with both parties. He knew of school policy and talked about positive relationships, the work in tutorials, and themes such as responsibility discussed in assemblies. His experience of policy in action had involved having been the instigator of a fight stopped by a member of staff who then attempted to find out what had happened. He said that most teachers could cope with such situations but some were better than others because they avoided humiliation – for him the most adverse feature of any incident in front of other people.

In reflecting on his behaviour, Chris argued that the most important thing was to stop fights happening again and he deplored intervention which failed to reach a conclusion which would be satisfactory to all parties. He saw this as leaving a way open for recriminations although he accepted that in order to have the last word there were frequently empty threats which were not then acted upon. The role of teachers in solving problems again came to the fore when Chris talked of the importance of 'trust' and that as they gain in maturity students ought to be left to resolve their own problems. Punishment was not necessary. It did nothing as a means of settling relationships because Chris believed that this put one of the parties in the wrong. Parents have an important part to play but again Chris felt that this needed to be fairly matched with both victim and bully supported by their parents, and he also thought that more support could be provided by the friends who could help you to think before you act. In his concluding comments, Chris said that he realized that there were principles which made for good relationships including being pleasant to others, but he stressed that this applied to the teaching staff and he argued that the 'image' of staff can affect the way students think about their situation in the school. To him the most important thing is to avoid losing face in any situation.

**Teasing**

This is a record of an interview with a boy, Andrew who, although teased from time to time about his height, regarded this as part of the social life of the group. As a result, he fitted into the normative category and does not accept that he was bullied; neither does he accept that he bullied others. He has a positive view of the school's anti-bullying policy and was one of the few interviewees who had an unequivocal view of teacher support.

### Andrew – Year 9

Andrew was a cheerful and sociable boy in Year 9, the first year of senior high school, and he felt that the school had provided a good framework for students to get on well with each other. Academically bright, he was however anxious to show that he was one of the crowd with enthusiasm for life with his mates, playing football and 'having a good laugh'. He was aware of the existence of some bullying within the school but had developed a direct approach of being firm with those who went beyond his limits for 'joking' and of offering help to others who he thought might be suffering from bullying. Although small in stature, and called 'titch' by others he felt that it was important for other students to know that he would not tolerate 'any bother'. Andrew's social network included several 'harder and older mates' who he felt he could call on if he needed help but he was keen to say that, so far in the school, it had not proved necessary because the teachers had been on the watch for potential trouble.

In reflecting on the anti-bullying policy of the school, Andrew spoke of three strengths. Teacher involvement had been balanced because there was no encouragement to 'grass' but year head, form tutor and subject teachers all seemed to know who the trouble-makers were and watched those who seemed to be unhappy to make sure that they were not being picked on. Andrew was also aware of the importance of assemblies and personal and social education in teaching students how to get along with each other and he recalled the emphasis on behaviour towards each other and letting people know what would happen if they were in the wrong. The third strength was that the system of sanctions began at the class level and this meant that most problems were coped with before they got out of hand. In his view 'it helped to show the difference between mucking about and real trouble because the serious cases get known and then get moved on to the year head, deputy head and head'.

Andrew felt that there were weaknesses in the way in which some of his friends reacted to young teachers and to new members of the school but he was keen to offer suggestions for improvements. He was also critical of the variation in class management techniques shown by some staff. To him, however, there was a known policy because it worked and things did get better, but he had never seen it written down – 'it is just the way they do things and we know what staff will do'.

> **Reflection**   How does 'the way in which we do things here' become
> ingrained in pupils? What does this suggest about the timing and
> type of intervention to change core values?

## The persistent bully

Some bullying behaviour is focused on one victim and is based upon
something which went wrong at an earlier stage in relationships. Debbie
presented an example of somebody who sustains physical and verbal
bullying of a girl in the group despite intervention by the staff of the school
and her own ability to rationalize her actions.

*Debbie – Year 9*

Debbie was in Year 9 – the first year of a senior high school and clearly had
problems both with work and social relationships. She showed a strong
streak of independence and felt alienated from the culture of the school
and resented staff expectations for her. Her 'liking for the lads' and her
view that she was 'no good in lessons' had led her to feel that she was not
wanted by the staff whom she believed were against her. She admitted to
physical and verbal bullying of a girl in the same group who had had problems whilst at middle school and who had then moved to another high
school only to transfer back in with her group after some weeks. The
verbal bullying took place all the while including class work situations,
and Debbie argued that this was because she had never got on with the
victim, but there was a more sinister element in that Debbie managed to
get other girls to support her and they had waited for the victim after
school when most physical bullying took place. To Debbie, such actions
were justified because of long-term hatred of the victim and the failure of
anyone in authority to listen to her side of the story. Fighting was acceptable behaviour and gave Debbie the chance to succeed.

   In talking about her behaviour and attitude, Debbie admitted that she
was acting counter to the policy of the school but felt that the attitude
shown to her by teachers worsened the situation. She listed 'having you in
their office and shouting at you without knowing the true story', 'teachers
should talk to pupils and listen to them after the lesson but they don't' and
although encouraged to talk to her form tutor she replied, 'not ours you
can't'. This had led her to be self-sufficient in coping with problems and
she felt that it was better to let the 'teachers threaten and shout and then
take the matter into your own hands after the lesson'. She accepted that
this prolonged the problem and took it out of the school but it was clear
that she wanted the last word in any situation. Debbie said that she would
go to her brothers and sisters before talking to her parents and she was

dismissive of those parents who went up to the school because they were too protective. She preferred her view that parents should let you manage your own affairs but that they should support you against others if 'you hit them one'. Whilst all this appeared negative Debbie argued for the appointment of a school counsellor who 'could listen without being part of the school staff. . . . someone who doesn't know what you are like in lessons and can't judge you by the way you work'.

## Coercion – the bully victim

Whilst there is a frequent admission to bullying behaviour in anonymous questionnaire responses interviewees were less ready to explore their behaviour with outsiders. This boy, John, explains some of the tensions which come with growing up and the need to be 'one of the lads' but at a cost of coercion if he is to remain as a member of a gang which exists outside school. The resultant behaviour showed characteristics of both bully and victim.

### John – Year 10

John was nearing the end of Year 10 when interviewed. He was described as mature, middle ability and streetwise with a group of friends who were older than himself including some who had left school. He was known amongst his year as a member of a 'hard' group and he admitted that he had used the protection which he believed they could give him to put pressure on younger students either to belittle them when 'mucking around, or to get things from them'. Membership of the group was important to John when out of school and he described the cost of this as having to be with them when there was extensive damage to property and several windows were broken. John was adamant that he was only a follower but in order to keep his standing when the others called him 'chicken' he took the blame in subsequent police action. He described the feelings of being pressured before he admitted involvement and then subsequently, of being 'used and run down' but he felt that he had to go along with the group to maintain his standing both in and out of school.

John seemed incapable of breaking away from the social grouping which was important to him. He spoke of his school experiences in a rather different way from others as a preparation for what occurs beyond school, either through knowing how to get along with others, or through being prepared for work because of good exam results. He was somewhat sceptical of teachers, mentioning their inconsistency in dealing with interpupil problems. Whilst he favoured teacher intervention and 'shaking on it' for petty arguments, he stressed that there was a need for greater toughness in the use of sanctions – expulsion presented no problems for him if serious bullying occurred. John saw the essential role of the teacher as ensuring that the victim was safe in any incident but he deplored any attempt to tell teachers what was happening because action which was attributable to 'grassing' would lead to retaliation out of school. He was however, prepared for parents to be involved because they had the ability to handle relationships outside the school gates. John was not aware of any school anti-bullying policies other than being told to 'behave yourself' and he was critical of attempts to introduce the subject in 'form time when everybody messes about'. He recalled a film on bullying but it was actually based on racism and this was not relevant to his own experience – he needed to know more about the way in which gangs developed.

### 'On the outside looking in'

These views are of one of those who might be considered as 'on the outside looking in'. The girl, Sarah, offered a series of comments which put bullying in perspective within the school but also spoke about the attitude of staff in a school which has a well-developed anti-bullying policy but where the emphasis placed on it by staff varies widely. Sarah also showed that increasing age brings with it greater reflective skills.

*Sarah – Year 10*

Sarah was in Year 10 in a large comprehensive school serving a mixed semi-urban and rural community. She believed that most students were friendly towards each other and that very little bullying actually occurred and that as one of the group she would help by sticking up for her friends if there was to be any breakdown in relationships. Her view was that there were occasional 'punch-ups' in any school but that most of the teasing and name calling was 'messing about' rather than bullying. She commented that there were staff who made a situation worse by either supporting the teasing to which some students were subjected, or by ignoring what was happening in class rather than confronting a problem head on. Sarah felt that the thought for the day and assembly teaching were of very limited value in settling any problems of relationships and that whilst there was a good structure for personal and social education in the school most teachers were unable to maintain the momentum and reverted to discussion which helped in that 'you get to know about people and it does help establish friendships but it does mean that whilst you learn that you aren't alone you don't do what the syllabus says'.

In reflecting on the way in which policies contributed to a happy school, Sarah commented that they were effective at a stage when a crisis occurred and the staff believed that something was important and it was 'all systems go'. She felt, however, that there was an inconsistency between the attitudes of different teachers and that 'to go ape over a petty thing' means that there was little impact when staff needed to act over something of major significance. To her, there was not sufficient attention paid to the management of the power of groups within the school. She felt that many of the problems which could result in bullying in other schools were overcome because the strength of friendship groupings within the school forced the small minority of bullies to 'back off', especially as the groups got older. Her narrative of an event where this occurred included reference to the belief that students were more successful at 'making people face things because they understand and they are at that point themselves'. She felt that staff failure to recognize this leads to unnecessary intervention which older students could control themselves. She also saw that intervention by parents, with or without invitation by the school, could lead to a worsening of the situation. Pupils could resolve matters if given the right situation but a situation deteriorates when those who are believed to have 'dobbed' are subject to a swing in student opinion. With balanced views, abundant self-confidence and maturity, Sarah was able to argue for some form of school court which would 'allow us to cope with problems at our level in a way which we understand'.

### The impact of maturity – overcoming past experiences

This sketch outlines the impact of increased maturity on the way in which a student handles a bullying situation. It shows how unhappy experiences in early adolescence were overcome. Whilst this might be related to a change of school, the social group is largely that which had operated in the middle school and improved relationships appear to have grown from positive efforts made by the girls themselves although obviously supported by parents, peers and staff. In this case, the past behaviour of the girl (Claire), accords with the victim/bully classification.

*Claire – Year 11*

Claire was in Year 11 at a senior high school. She was a bright girl and enjoyed a sociable life with a wide range of friends. To her, friends were important as support and help, in fostering the development of social skills and in learning how to communicate. She had an unhappy time whilst at middle school when there were problems with another girl who was herself upset because Claire appeared to be able to establish better relationships with the boys in the group. Bullying at that time took the form of verbal abuse, attempts to have Claire excluded from the social grouping and petty interference with property. This was upsetting and eventually Claire told her mother of events and between them they sorted out a policy of facing the bully and endeavouring to talk the problem through. This proved to be a successful approach and Claire has now maintained her friendship with the former bully over a period of 18 months. During the period in which she was bullied she admitted that she felt miserable and that she may have reacted adversely against others either through verbal aggression or by attempts at social exclusion of other group members because she was so unhappy – 'it was an attempt to get her own back'.

Claire does not appear to be a true bully / victim. She admitted that she had reacted to her own unhappiness but her reflection shows that the intent was rarely premeditated and was most frequently a spontaneous attempt to maintain her standing within the group. The action was not continuous and Claire would now be seen as one of the normative group for whom bullying is anathema. Her view was that this was a stage of growing up and that she subsequently enjoyed easy relationships with a wide group of friends. She was convinced that similar problems in the future could be overcome through 'talking things out in the open' and had the confidence to manage such a situation without other inter-vention.

When reflecting on the experience, Claire was clear that the role of par-ents was initially to listen and she outlined the experience of another girl for whom 'parents came down to school with all guns blazing, and it just didn't work that way'. It may be that school could act as a facilitator so that the parents concerned can talk events through with the students in a struc-tured way with available mediation. Claire felt that teacher involvement had to be carefully managed and cites, as an example, one teacher who, when intervening made bully and victim stand on chairs and then attempted to subdue the bully by embarrassing her in front of the group – to her, this merely postponed the final reckoning to a place and time away from school and with no ready support. She showed the effect of increased maturity by wanting colleagues and staff to work towards a situation where good relationships between students were the main aim of any policy. She was sceptical of the way in which the matter of relationships was handled in social education because 'it was out of a book and wasn't really a help' and felt that whilst she would talk to her form teacher, there were some staff to whom she would not turn. Although not in a school which offered peer counselling she suggested that some training for older students could be helpful because 'you will talk to someone more or less your own age that you can trust'. Claire was also keen to encourage social activities in a common room away from the playground environment but the large numbers of sixth formers put a pressure on suitable inside accommodation and their existence appeared to delay the maturation of the Year 11 cohort.

### The impact of maturity – growing self-confidence

This outline of a discussion shows how students mature and develop a broader view of bullying behaviour. Jason felt that he was a victim for part of Year 10 and reflects upon the tension between his view of himself as part of the group and the efforts of the school to combat anti-social behaviour. Increasing maturity led him to feel that it is better to grow in self-confidence rather than rely upon staff intervention.

*Jason – Year 11*

Jason was in his final year in an 11–16 mixed comprehensive in an inner urban school. He was a solid worker and felt that he had become popular with a group of friends who shared his interests in lunch-time and after-school clubs and activities including sport and information technology. He spoke of the school as a friendly place with good relationships with the staff and with other students but he admitted that this situation had only come about during the past year as he 'settled in with a new group of friends'. He had had a run of friends in the lower school but then fell out with his group in Year 10. The reasons for this appear to be connected with his frustration at immature behaviour and teasing which he felt was getting in the way of progress with his work. The need to work without others realizing that you are working had been a constant anxiety especially as he was keen to do well to meet parental expectations for him. This together with awareness that he was being marginalized by the group of former friends led him to feel most unhappy. The 'loneliness of being on the fringe of things and without any apparent friends was pretty awful especially when you lose the ability to talk to others because you are frightened that they will reject you too'. The solution to his problem appears to have come from discussion in social education during Year 10 when 'people seemed to grow up, they were more ready to listen to other viewpoints and the staff pushed everybody to get on with each other and with the work we needed for the exams'.

In looking at the situation, Jason felt that teachers could have been more aware of his unhappiness and that he had not been doing as well as he ought because of this, but he was aware of the problem of 'ensuring that staff do more but with minimal intervention'. He was particularly critical of attempts to improve situations by moving students to different groups where there was then a new problem in making friendships, and he felt that the practice of referral of all serious matters to senior staff created difficulties by breaking confidences and opening the situation to widespread discussion and comment from staff who are not involved. To him, it was a matter of staff giving active support but allowing the student, especially as he or she gets older, to manage the situation within personal parameters. Jason felt that students exacerbate difficult situations because of a tendency to gossip and exaggerate and he gave an example of a girl who attempted to overdose, who was then pointed out by others when matters ought to have been handled between school and parents alone. Nevertheless, in his last weeks at school Jason welcomed open discussion of an extension to the anti-bullying policy by the staff setting out a series of procedures offering help in crisis, curriculum, and counselling situations. He felt though, that more needed to be done to move decision-making and action to student level especially in developing good relationships and he argued for an effective school council.

## Attaining maturity

Whilst the eight students detailed above do not provide sufficient evidence upon which to base a theory of development, their experience and reflections suggest that they are subject to a sequential maturation process which may be helped forward by school policies. Boulton and Underwood (1992) investigated the social behaviour of six classes of middle-school children and established the view that bullies believe that their behaviour arises from provocation by others, but in reality they are responding to a self-perception that they are hard or tough, and actually lack empathy for those who are different from themselves in physical, cultural or socio-economic ways. By contrast, the victims are lacking in self-esteem, a situation which is worsened as a result of bullying, and again this may be related to the external deviations outlined by Olweus (1993). Boulton (1994) also outlines the behaviour of bullies, victims, and 'not involved', among 8–10-year-old boys in the school playground. He characterizes bullies as likely to move in groups, and to be more involved in team and rule games, whilst victims tend to be loners, to be those who have more intense but limited relationships and to be those who avoid rule games. The 1992 research established that girls were likely to be later participating in teasing or bullying activities but that to the victims the effects were no less distressing than for the boys. Drouet (1993) has examined the nature of bullying amongst girls and shows how a combination of differential maturation, lack of self-confidence as a result of underdevelopment, or overdevelopment, and sexual harassment, even between girls, leads to misery for many students, including as Newton (1993) shows, within the fee-paying sector.

By the start of sixth form or further education, however, most students believe that they are neither bully nor victim and that they have the confidence needed to cope with comment from colleagues on the way in which differing work patterns, appearance and social networks mark one individual from another. This may be related to the sifting process which occurs at the end of Year 11, and to the consequent reforming of work groups either within school or further education. The evidence from the USA where the progression towards aged 18 years is more uniform is that maturation is a slower process and physical size results in more violent bullying activities for both boys and girls for a longer period (Mulhern 1994).

---

**Reflection**    Does the age of automatic seniority, i.e. 16 in an 11–16 school, 18 in an 11–18 school, affect staff and pupil attitudes to behaviour? How should this be recognized in developing policies?

---

This complex progression from middle school to sixth form is evident in the behaviour of students detailed in this chapter. Problems of transition, whether at 11 or 13 years, are made more intense where physical development, appearance, and physical or academic ability traits lead to dominance by the bully, and loss of confidence by the bullied. Shakeshaft (1995) refers to this as 'peer harassment' which he argues is unrelated to race or gender but is more likely to cut across groupings. At this time, girls appear to be more ready to use verbal and exclusive bullying to belittle other girls, especially those from differing background or social grouping, but attention then swings to posturing over relationships with boys especially where their out-of-school social life is with a more sophisticated group. Boys at this stage have more readily identified gang allegiances beyond the school limits and the bullies are marked by 'hardness'; the victims by their physical distress and lack of friends. However, during the mid-adolescent period the power of the non-aligned normative group gradually takes effect as shown by the comments of the older interviewees who are prepared to see that the way in which teaching staff have managed events in school, and the cumulative effect of social education together with the increased willingness of peers to discuss and listen, results in an improved environment. This may indicate that physical maturity is matched by social competence as explored by Holmes (1995), but it may show that students are more able to maintain their own security by avoiding those interrelationships which bring them into contact with adverse comment or action. This is suggested as the reason for the decline in reported bullying in the senior years of US high schools (Chandler 1995).

All of the interviewees detailed in this chapter are white European and none of the interviews led to detailing of racism or gender harassment. Whilst some of the students did not recognize the existence of anti-bullying policies they were all aware that there would be serious repercussions from teachers if there was evidence of overtly racist or sexist bullying. However, there is some evidence from the open comment sections of questionnaires that those from minority ethnic groups do still suffer from overt racism outside school and more surreptitious distress in some school situations. There is no doubt that some of the respondents do feel unhappy because their religion, race or gender form the butt of comment from other students. For them, there is a differing self-image within the school community than that which is maintained within the home where they are insulated from external cultures.

# 3 | GETTING ON WITH OTHERS

## Introduction

In Chapter 2, we suggested that the development of self-image within an atmosphere which offers security appears to be fundamental to a progression from polarized victim or bully behaviour to a mature self-confidence and the ability to handle relationships. The Keele Partnership investigation was concerned to find out something of the way in which students develop their ability to get along with others. The findings offer an insight into the motivation which conditions the nature of interstudent relationships either as individuals, subgroups or groups, and suggest areas of these relationships which should become a focus of behavioural improvement.

Although there is a fair representation of each secondary year group the timing of the administration of the questionnaire resulted in a range of responses from a maximum of 16 per cent of Year 11 to 25 per cent of Year 9 in the 25 schools. There were no marked ethnic groups although the 87 per cent white European, and main Asian subgroup of 2 per cent may be distorted by the exclusion of the 9 per cent who preferred not to say anything about their background. Responses came from 51 per cent males and 49 per cent females matched consistently across all year groups. The predominant white European nature of the sample may have distorted findings if compared with schools in other areas of the UK. Loach and Bloor (1994) and Siann (1994) for example, suggest that whilst students would argue otherwise, there is a tendency for bullying to be a cover for more deep-rooted racism – a factor of importance in establishing a balanced focus for anti-bullying education. Similar investigations of the relationship between gender and susceptibility to bullying and victimization (Boulton and Underwood 1992; Stein 1995) indicate that during a period of physical bullying, boys may attack boys, that girls may attack weak boys or girls, but that few girls are attacked by boys. As verbal bullying becomes more widespread both boys and girls will harass the other gender. Anti-bullying education has, therefore, to be concerned with gender issues.

The data showed something of the family background of the sample. The majority of respondents were from two- or three-children families (73 per cent), 7 per cent were only children and 10 per cent came from families with more than five children. Replies were fairly well spread between the eldest, the youngest and those in between, although there was a tendency for the respondents in Years 10 and 11 to be the eldest. Financial circumstances are indicated by the fact that 11 per cent of respondents took free school meals, and a further 6 per cent were entitled to do so. The percentage not entitled to free meals (83 per cent) is slightly above the national average and may indicate a marginally above average standard of living although the difference between individual schools is greater than the statistical norm for the group as a whole suggests and one school in the sample has a 44 per cent free-meal entitlement.

In his earliest work, Olweus (1978) suggested that because of the apparently high level of agreement in student and staff identification of bullying activity, it might be accepted as part of the normal life of the school and comments such as 'it always happens when you get a crowd together', 'they have to go through this phase' and 'some students just ask for it' indicate that some staff have developed stereotypical views of behaviour. These stereotypes also exist in the views of the victim as a student who is socially inept, having problems with communication with adults and peers, self-centred, introvert, inflexible but attention-seeking (Lowenstein 1978a,b), and of the bully as a child of bullying parents, physically strong, lacking sensitivity, disruptive in class and often involved in truancy or criminal activities. Subsequent work has refined these views both because bullying is more widespread than originally thought, and also because it appears to have become more subtle in form. Anti-bullying measures have therefore, to support complex behavioural change. This is particularly so in considering the ability levels of students. A typical pattern of victims of lower intelligence and brighter aggressors is now questioned. Byrne (1994a) and Thompson *et al.* (1994b) have shown how mainstream integration of students with special learning needs has led to a modification of the reported bullying which occurs when segregation is the norm. When students are socially integrated and this is supported by personal and social education and some opportunity to pull away from the crowd, the lesser intelligent appear to thrive.

**Reflection**   How is our thinking about aspects of bullying behaviour affected by stereotypical views of bullies and victims? Has our own background and experience affected this?

Because so much of the evidence from this earlier research had shown the relationship between bullying behaviour and personal characteristics, the pupils were asked how they fitted certain physical and personality criteria. In each of these criteria students classify themselves as average or better than average more readily than they believe that they are below average – as shown by 25 per cent being tall for their age but only 16 per cent being small, and 48 per cent considering that their abilities are high average or better, with only 5 per cent as low average or worse. The reality might be nearer the figure for maths sets with 41 per cent in a high set, and 14 per cent in a low set but self-esteem is an important factor in coping with school situations and our respondents clearly have a higher opinion of themselves than subsequent evidence from other pupils suggests. Factors in developing self-esteem include: height, affecting 41 per cent; weight problems affecting 28 per cent; ability levels, with 5 per cent believing that they are below average, and a range of disabilities of which poor eyesight, asthma and acne are each claimed as problems by over 25 per cent of the cohort. Gender analysis shows that perceptions of being overweight affect 22 per cent of the girls, compared with 14 per cent of the boys but in all other respects there is no significant difference.

## Why bully?

We sought evidence of the nature and frequency of bullying but as the respondents could only report on their own situation, the evidence for any change as a result of policy development has to be deduced from comparison with other projects. Students were not asked whether they were bullies but whether they had taken part in listed behaviours. Thus many who would not say that they were actually bullies admitted to aggressive, taunting or intimidating behaviour. The motivation to bully was explored generally by seeking views on participation in anti-social behaviour, and specifically by assessing the reasons for discrimination. Overall, 53 per cent feel that there are rarely or never good reasons for fighting in school but this masks a figure of 46 per cent of boys and 60 per cent of the girls. This sustains the evidence that boys are more physical in their bullying (Marano 1995). The girls are also more sympathetic to victims with 55 per cent aware that picking on a person is never or rarely deserved, whilst only 45 per cent of boys believe that this is so. The data do show some change over time as students absorb a new culture following a change of school. There is an increase of 11 per cent in the number of those who believe that fighting is justified between Year 7 and Year 8, and there is then a hard core of about a quarter of students feeling that this is so until there is a slight fall in Year 11. At this stage, there are more who feel that fighting is sometimes justified indicating a more pragmatic approach to relationships.

**Table 3.1** Factors in discrimination against other students

| Factor | Male (n = 1793) (%) | Female (n = 1624) (%) | Total (n = 3417) (%) |
|---|---|---|---|
| Personal | | | |
| ethnic group | 8 | 2 | 6 |
| gender | 8 | 5 | 7 |
| religion | 9 | 4 | 6 |
| disability | 8 | 5 | 7 |
| physical size | 6 | 4 | 5 |
| Socio-economic | | | |
| family | 3 | 2 | 3 |
| being rich | 7 | 4 | 6 |
| being poor | 6 | 3 | 5 |
| where they live | 4 | 2 | 3 |
| School attitudes | | | |
| hard work | 9 | 6 | 8 |
| learning problems | 8 | 4 | 6 |
| too clever | 14 | 12 | 13 |
| no good at sport | 8 | 4 | 6 |
| Being different | | | |
| looks | 14 | 13 | 13 |
| dress | 16 | 18 | 17 |
| new to school | 7 | 5 | 6 |
| Some other reason | 61 | 71 | 66 |

The factors which cause people to discriminate against others to the point of bullying are varied and outlined in Table 3.1. Respondents were allowed to list as many of these factors as they felt relevant in their situation. The range for any factor is between 3 per cent and 17 per cent, but significantly 66 per cent felt that the reason for discrimination was not amongst those listed.

Interview data suggests that the reason for discrimination may never be rationally explained as shown in the comments 'I hadn't got on with her ever since primary school . . . I don't know why', and 'it's the way he looks at me makes me feel I don't like him'. Some interfamily feuding determines attitudes as where 'we aren't allowed to mix with them' or 'he has a reputation of being from a hard family'. Many of the responses were a rationalization but the real cause appears to have been a reaction to past events. The most common of these were relationships (63 per cent of the narratives), a failure to comply with peer pressures (14 per cent of the narratives) and 'showing that we are hard and that we can make them part of our gang' which affected both boys and girls in Years 9 and 10. Where reasons are teased out, the following pattern of discriminatory behaviour emerges:

- *Personal* – ethnic background and religion are more frequently mentioned amongst the older males in the older age groups whilst gender is most frequently mentioned reason for discrimination in the earlier secondary years and as a male taunt.
- *Socio-economic* – area of residence, perceptions of being rich or poor and family background are consistently of limited concern but the way people look and the way in which they dress is most significant overall and especially for the girls.
- *School attitudes* – hard workers are attacked by boys more than girls but less so in the older years, but obvious cleverness invokes more marked criticism for both boys and girls until Year 11. Learning problems and lack of sporting aptitude are deprecated by boys more consistently than by girls but both become more tolerant by Year 11.
- *Being different* – causes 10 per cent to discriminate with little evidence of increased tolerance with age and this is shown in evidence of 'speaking poshly' which is consistently attacked as also is being new to the school which also affects the attitude of 6 per cent of the respondents, although girls are more inclined to be helpful in this respect.

It is not possible to say whether identification of the reasons for discrimination is helpful in changing student attitudes. Narratives show that early intervention, usually in Years 7 and 8, may lead to squabbles being settled and friendships then developing, but it seems that 'some people never will get along and the only thing you can do is hope for genetic change' and, as a result avoidance of problems in relationships as shown by the comment that

> this is a happy school and I enjoy being here because it is big enough to let you keep away from people you don't want to mix with . . . as a person who comes on the bus from the villages there are some girls who only want to tease you because they think you are posh but I can keep away from them.

## Physical bullying

Whether students have developed a different vocabulary and now see what was formerly classed as horse-play as bullying is difficult to judge from the evidence. Discussion amongst classes shows that any attempt to interfere with others, or to cause them unhappiness is seen as bullying but there is some difference between those who admit that they have hurt others in the past year and the admission of types of physical action which could be seen as bullying. Those who admit to bullying behaviour at some time in the past year reach 75 per cent of the cohort, the victims with experience of all types of bullying total 74 per cent. This indicates that the students have a similar view of behaviour. However, there are variations in the perceived frequency and type of bullying for example, whilst 40 per cent of 3411 respondents think that they have been threatened with violence, 35 per cent of 3177 believe that they acted in this way. The interviews revealed a perception by peers that there are a group of people who are both victim and bully. Analysis of the narratives given in interviews suggests that this small group, about 7 per cent of the total, have developed their attitude because of 'the need to stand up for yourself', 'to show that you are as hard as those who pick on you', 'to be one of the gang' and 'because my brother was hard I got picked on and then had to be hard too'. The open comments show a considerable degree of understanding by some pupils:

> Sometimes people are bullied by their friends. Then their friends punch them pretending it was a joke when they really meant it to hurt.

> Most of the people who bully are people who are not as good as someone at something . . . this induces a feeling of anger in the person who lashes out physically or verbally due to their insecurity. This can probably never be prevented because you'll always get people who are better at things than others, and you will always get people who feel that the only way to get some recognition is to make fun of others. Some people however, bully because they have been bullied. This revenge can cause a vicious circle.

---

**Reflection**   How can the tension between the 'have and have-nots' be influenced by staff attitudes and actions?

---

Cultural norms appear to have affected admissions of the type of bullying in the readier acceptance that 67 per cent say that they had pushed, and 38 per cent said that they had punched others, but only 56 per cent, and 34 per cent, respectively, say that they have suffered this. The converse is seen in that only 9 per cent admit to sexual touching, but 15 per cent believe that this has happened to them, and 9 per cent admit to spitting but 16 per cent believe that they have been victims of this behaviour. The power of intimidation is shown in that only 15 per cent thought that they had made others fight but 27 per cent believed that this had been incumbent upon them – a feature of younger males and older females. Acts of physical violence have been seen often or more frequently by 27 per cent of the respondents but this includes playground fights which in the view of one interviewee were 'not really bullying because it is out in the open, proper fighting!'

In physical terms, pushing, tripping and punching have been experienced by over one-third of all pupils at some stage in the past year. Threatening with violence may have been a precursor to actual physical violence but 40 per cent of victims who had been bullied believe that they may have deflected further action as the narratives outlined in the interviews showed – 'they were just being hard', 'they wanted to show the others they were big' and 'she wanted to set me up' being some of the reasoning suggested. Seven per cent said that they physically bullied often or more frequently, and 29 per cent said that they did so 'sometimes'. Mistreatment includes pushing admitted by over two-thirds (67 per cent), tripping (36 per cent), punching (39 per cent) and kicking (29 per cent). The gender differences are shown in Table 3.2. The behaviours appear to be consistent across the age ranges except that punching and kicking become more obvious amongst the older pupils. However, there are significant differences in behaviour between the genders – the girls being more ready to slap (30 per cent), and pull hair (17 per cent) but less likely to punch or kick. Sexual offensiveness is slightly more likely to be an act of older males. Comparisons indicate that the overall bullying figure of 7 per cent is comparable with the admissions made by students in the Olweus (1983) secondary school survey, but far less than the 42 per cent of pupils actually observed in incidents in classes in Sheffield in 1988 (Ahmad and Smith 1990). A comparison between admitted behaviours and experienced mistreatment shows that rather more (6 per cent) admit to bullying than to being mistreated. This may arise from interpretation of the degree of hurt suffered, but it may also reflect that some accidental mistreatment is accepted as such by the victims. This is shown in that 29 per cent of the respondents

**Table 3.2** Nature of physical bullying admitted by respondents ($n = 3386$)

| Mistreatment of others | Male (%) | Female (%) | Total (%) |
| --- | --- | --- | --- |
| Threatened with violence | 40 | 29 | 35 |
| Pushed | 66 | 69 | 67 |
| Pulled by the hair | 7 | 17 | 12 |
| Slapped | 8 | 30 | 18 |
| Punched | 51 | 22 | 38 |
| Sexual touching | 11 | 7 | 9 |
| Kicked | 35 | 22 | 29 |
| Tripped | 41 | 28 | 36 |
| Stamped on | 12 | 5 | 9 |
| Spat on | 11 | 6 | 9 |
| Made to fight | 19 | 9 | 15 |

thought that they had kicked others whereas only 5 per cent thought that they had been kicked. That said, there is a remarkable consistency between admission and experience of types of physical bullying.

Discussion with staff in the project schools showed a range of opinion from those who believed that any physical contact had to be seen as an incursion into another student's private space to those who believed that horse-play was a feature of growing up. Van Acker (1995) defines four types of violence within schools:

- *situational*, arising from the heat of the moment;
- *relationship*, arising from inability to get along with one or more colleagues;
- *predatory*, arising from the use of dominating behaviour by a bully over a range of victims; and
- *psychopathological*, that connected with serious behavioural problems.

Analysis of the school staff comments shows that there is a tendency for staff to accept situational violence – the playground fight – as requiring different handling to other failures in relationship. This is also reflected in student comment:

> having a scrap is not serious . . . it's just how we grow up and some of the teachers know this, so that if there is trouble they stop the fight and then give people time to cool down and then they talk about it . . . others go over the top when it is a little thing.

Students are aware that problems in relationships may require longer term staff intervention as in the situation where:

> it has been difficult to get on with one of the girls in my class but the form teacher knows this and avoids us having to be in the same group for things . . . I could change my class but I don't want to do so until the end of the year because it will get in the way of my work.

Predatory violence has no place in the catalogue of acceptable behaviour for most interviewees except when the bullying becomes a group behaviour outlined by one victim in the following way:

> the pupils mostly go around in gangs of boys, teasing and picking on one person, mostly a boy, until he says something or stand up to them and then they all pile on him.

Bentley and Li (1995) have investigated the behaviour of the non-bully or other victims in this situation and found a readiness for these to support the bullies in those situations where they were not personally involved – in the words of one interviewee 'there are times when they get me, but at times I go along with them so that they know that I can be as hard as they are'.

## Teasing and taunting

Interview evidence showed that there were comparatively few pupils who felt that there was much physical bullying within their school – except for pupils from two of the twenty-five schools. The frequency of physical hurt at 3 per cent for 'often' and 3 per cent 'very often' appears similarly low. However, there is a difference between the 1774 who say that they have been physically hurt in the past year and the 3177 who have suffered the full range of physical taunts but without incurring injury. Does this suggest that some of the taunting has an emotional rather than a physical hurt value? Comments from individuals suggest that this might be so:

> I was called names and pushed about – it just made me feel very lonely.

> They threatened to beat me up and crowded me in – it made me feel very lonely.

> Lindsey was hit by one of the other girls who had also been insulting her – it just made her very angry.

The dynamics are shown in the following open comment:

> I feel that at our school there is mostly verbal bullying but when you try to answer back there is more tension and then an outburst of violence which is a lot of trouble.

This reflects the observations undertaken by Boulton (1993) where aggressive reaction amongst middle-school children resulted from teasing, disagreements over games, dislike and dominance disputes. As substantiated in the narratives for the Keele Partnership research the commonest causes of fights were an aggressive reaction to teasing, or after accidental injury.

Recent research highlights the shift of student perception of bullying as more frequently verbal taunting rather than physical harm. If physical bullying is to be controlled student attitudes to teasing and verbal taunts have also to be changed. Hoover (1993) found that in a group of middle-school children although 90 per cent felt that they had been bullied, teasing was the most common behaviour. The interview and open comment in the Keele Partnership investigation shows that there is a growing tension between student belief that teachers should help curb teasing and the reality of this control. 'Teachers turn a blind eye to name calling because they believe it doesn't hurt you', 'it seems that action is only taken if somebody is really hurt' and 'teachers want a school with no bullying and so they pretend it doesn't exist', are all perceptive comments from younger students.

Besides teasing and verbal bullying, there has been an apparent increase in theft and damage to belongings as a means of causing distress to others.

Whilst the nature of teasing was not detailed, 24 per cent of respondents felt that they were teased often or very often. There is a tendency for boys to report this more frequently than the girls. It seems that teasing increases as students settle into the school (Year 7 figures indicate 24 per cent as 'often or very often' victims rising to 29 per cent in Year 8), but then settle back with maturity dropping to 16 per cent in Year 11. Sometimes for a further 28 per cent, teasing seriously undermines pupils' feelings of security. Fifty-two per cent of pupils report witnessing incidents often or very often and interview evidence shows that this is a feature of the pupil culture in many schools where 'they say things as you move up the stairs – "slag", "bitch", that sort of thing' or where 'they pick on you for some reason like your height and laugh at this even in class'. Interview evidence and open comment both indicate that the spreading of lies and rumours has often or very often affected about 22 per cent of the respondents with a tendency for it to occur more frequently in Years 9 and 10. Contrary to comments of staff and interviewees who think that this is more likely to be a feature of female behaviour, the questionnaire evidence shows that it is rather more likely to occur with males in Years 7 and 8, and then with females in Years 9 and 10. A summary of rationale and impact is offered in one open comment:

> In our school it is more verbal bullying than physical, and bitching behind people's backs, rumour spreading and things like that. If you're being talked about it could be because of anything. It doesn't matter if you're fat or thin, pretty or ugly – you could be picked on because you're pretty and have a nice figure, just because people are jealous of you. There is no discrimination sometimes. Just if someone takes a dislike to you they make your life hell.

Taunting often involves interference with personal property. The most common admissions are to taking somebody else's bag (26 per cent), breaking someone's property (44 per cent) and damaging school books belonging to another pupil (24 per cent). The interviews suggest that many of these are connected 'with an attempt to be hard' or 'to get them to do something they might not want to do'. Whilst the percentages of those admitting damage are comparable it does seem that girls are less likely to break personal goods but more likely to do so to school property. This is explained as 'getting at a person without actually damaging their stuff – it isn't quite as bad'. The 931 students admitting theft and property damage can be compared with 1419 pupils who have suffered these incidents. This might be because 'it becomes a habit with some people who do it to make their mark' but it may also be that 'some of the kids believe that they have been bullied when people are mucking around – especially if it happens in class'. Nevertheless, 21 per cent of the cohort have had items of property damaged frequently, again without always regarding this as bullying activity. The prevalence of perceived damage to property (47 per cent), school bag taking (26 per cent) and damage to school books (21 per cent) does however, reflect the figures given by bullies. Whilst there is a consistency about the occurrence of these events between male and female respondents, except that males are three times more likely than females to demand dinner tickets, there is a variation in behaviour across the years. In general, property damage is reported more frequently amongst older pupils, but damage to kit and clothes, and demands for money are much more likely in the younger secondary years.

The misery can be judged by one of the open comments:

> Other pupils in school take my pens and pencils and break them. They used to throw them out of the windows. They put my school bag out of the window once when it was raining and it went into a puddle. When I started in Year 8 I spent £11 on new pens – now I hardly have any. They say if you tell on them they will beat you up.

Another girl felt that:

> people treat others badly if they are different in any way . . . for example they tease you if you have things which aren't as good as theirs.

This is an echo of the misery of non-uniform days for some students where 'they get at you if what you are wearing is not one of the in names'.


## 'Out in the cold'

Exclusion from social groupings is also seen as a pernicious non-verbal behaviour which often or very often causes unhappiness for a total of 11 per cent of respondents. Although slightly more likely for a girl, it is nevertheless a source of misery to boys, one of whom commented:

> I was in the football team and we lost – they thought that it was partly down to me and so they started shunning me – I didn't feel that I belonged and then I didn't want to go to school because I wasn't happy there any more.

The impact of social exclusion is most graphically described by girls, one of whom states that:

> everything was all right until I was ill – when I went back to school the girls had made new friends and they didn't want me – this made me feel unhappy so that I didn't want to go to school and I knew that it was because of a strong ringleader.

Interview evidence indicates that volatile friendships are more likely to be a feature of the junior secondary years, but in later adolescence social exclusion is more likely to be a permanent feature of life for some students usually where 'a person is different because of what he or she looks like or how he or she behaves or even how they get on with work, but you can't make people be friendly'. There is evidence from the practice of schools which are obviously successful in maintaining social interaction that attitudes can be changed and being different becomes a positive attribute. Arora (1994), has shown how assertiveness training can empower some students in this situation.

---

**Reflection** What are the likely consequences of more assertive behaviour for victims who may appear to pupils and staff to be changing their character or personality? How can this be managed?

---

### Getting older, or getting wiser?

There has been an implicit view that either, or both, maturation and anti-bullying education have an effect on student attitudes to bullying. This is certainly borne out in the fall in numbers of students experiencing various bullying activities as shown in Table 3.3.

It is also possible that students are less affected by bullying because they develop avoidance strategies. In considering 6500 high-school student responses in the USA, Chandler (1995) has shown that half of the cohort take measures such as remaining with a group, avoiding part of the school buildings, using routes where they are sure of supervision and, at the extreme, avoiding school. The interview and open comment evidence shows this to be also true in some schools in the current sample – 'I don't go home until most of the others have gone and I am sure that it is safe to do so', 'it is better if you can keep away from the cycle sheds because that

**Table 3.3** Change in reported bullying behaviour experienced by age group

| Behaviour experienced* | Number of pupils | Age group (years) | | | | |
|---|---|---|---|---|---|---|
| | | 7(%) | 8(%) | 9(%) | 10(%) | 11(%) |
| Suffered untruths | 4305 | 22 | 25 | 22 | 22 | 17 |
| Socially excluded | 4380 | 16 | 12 | 11 | 9 | 8 |
| Physically hurt | 4355 | 9 | 8 | 7 | 3 | 2 |
| Property damaged | 4323 | 8 | 8 | 6 | 8 | 5 |
| Teasing and abuse | 4312 | 24 | 29 | 27 | 23 | 16 |

* Often or very often in year

is where the smokers meet up and they think that you will grass' and 'the best thing to do is to get into a gang . . . not a bad gang but a group who will help you'. Garrity (1994) suggests that the long-term effect of anti-bullying policies is achieved through the 'mobilisation of the silent majority' and there is evidence that some schools are using this as a way forward mirrored in individual comment that 'at our school pupils are pretty cool to each other and this is influenced by the teachers' help' and 'I have only ever had one problem with other pupils and it was sorted out as soon as possible when I told the teachers'. At the same time, there are many comments which indicate that teachers are seen to be inept and that many situations are improved as a result of 'realizing that I was not going to get anywhere unless I stood up to them and when they knew that I was getting help from my gang, not really a bad group, it all disappeared'. Social maturity is frequently enhanced by out-of-school relationships shown in comments about 'knowing that my older friends would wait for her after school if she kept up the aggro' and 'I have several friends who are older than I am and I rely on them to help me'.

Some elements of being different, however, do not change as students get older. Gordon (1992) stresses the relative isolation of students from ethnic minorities in rural and semirural schools, and the evidence from the current research shows that there is a spectrum with those who are well integrated and for whom 'they never talk about my colour because they know that I am as English as they are' to those who 'always suffer because they think that I don't live the sort of life they live and so I get a lot of abuse in an underhand way'. Within the urban schools where racial groupings are more significant, tensions develop between groups. Whilst these are contained within school and 'we have to get along most of the time', there is antipathy in out-of-school situations resulting in 'going for the coloured kids because they aren't really part of our community'. Disability appears to be more easily understood as students get older and protective groupings form to emphasize the attitudes of tolerance and support which are developed in drama and social education in one school which 'is a caring school and we all try to get on with each other and have a lot of pressure to help those with difficulties'. In another school where transition from middle school is at the age of 13 years, sixth-form mentors are used as advocates for younger pupils with learning problems during their induction year with training to help sponsor social integration.

## Out of sight, out of mind?

Fostering positive social relationships requires awareness of the areas where things can go wrong. The Sheffield project (Smith and Sharp 1994) indicated that bullying activity is generated wherever pupils are together

**Table 3.4** Location of bullying activity ($n$ = 1900 males, 1700 females)

| Location | Physical | | Teasing and abuse | |
|---|---|---|---|---|
| | Male (%) | Female (%) | Male (%) | Female (%) |
| Out of school | 58 | 63 | 34 | 32 |
| Playground | 46 | 40 | 51 | 39 |
| Corridors | 17 | 21 | 28 | 28 |
| Dining room | 6 | 4 | 14 | 13 |
| During lessons | 19 | 15 | 16 | 19 |

and that the classroom, as the principal area of interaction was not immune from this. Responses in the Keele Partnership investigation show that this is still true with 21 per cent of reported physical bullying, and 50 per cent of teasing occurring in the classroom. Table 3.4 gives the detail of the location of bullying activity.

Indeed, the comments from interviewees suggest that 'some teachers are just not able to do anything about it', 'some teachers pretend not to see so that they can get on with the lesson', 'the weaker teachers are frightened of the bully in our class' and 'it is only when you have strict teachers and they keep us down to work that I enjoy my lesson because I won't get picked on'. The experience of 45 per cent of the respondents in the playground areas is clearly not happy in some schools with 'lack of teacher supervision', 'the way in which gangs can get you without anybody else seeing' and 'the hard girls decide to pick on somebody and then make her life hell but to the outside world it looks as if a group are talking together'. Slee (1995) has detailed the experience in Australian schools and shows that there is a tendency for physical bullying to be more obvious where the relatively open spaces allow pupils to gather away from supervision. Whilst the teasing prevails in the dining room and corridors, physical bullying is much less obvious in these areas of the school where staff supervision is more effective. Boys appear to suffer more in the playgrounds, and girls on the school corridors, but both boys and girls suffer similarly out of school which is the principal location for physical attacks. These are 'often when the gang gets together and then waits for you', 'when girls are set up to fight because it is not as easy at school', 'when the staff have gone back in after we have all left' and 'when they wait for you even though you stay at school to do things'. It seems that teasing is less prevalent, although still affecting one-quarter of the respondents, out of school. For the rural schools this is obviously more of a problem on the school buses where 'who you are and where you live is obvious to those who make your life difficult'.

## Impact

Whatever the type of bullying, there is evidence that it causes schooling to be an unpleasant experience for many students. A group of 11 per cent feel excluded, 6 per cent endure frequent physical mistreatment and 7 per cent suffer property damage, and the comments interviewees make show the need for action to improve this situation.

> I get treated badly because my dad works at my school . . . I have told someone [form tutor] but he said to ignore them, but you can't when it hurts.

> I feel that home life and school life is no good and I can't wait to leave both of them because not one of them is fair.

Whilst these indicate that some students have a continual battle, a summary of the situation by one Year 11 student maintains the perspective which leads to the conclusion that bullying, whilst a problem, is being contained for most students in most of the schools in our sample.

> We do have racists here, not many but they tend to keep it quiet, not bully the coloured people face on . . . Sometimes people don't realize they are hurting someone, they could be just joking around, not meaning it seriously but still doing damage. Popular people tend to bully here to boost their big egos and to make themselves look better . . . sometimes there are really nice people hiding beneath an exterior which society considers to be ugly, but people don't want to know them because of the way they look. I think that something has gone wrong in society and that we value the wrong things.

These comments are from students in schools where there is a commitment to anti-bullying policies. Despite carefully structured interventions problems continue. Olweus (1994) accepts that even after 8–20 months, there may only be limited change – nevertheless, in the right direction. Peplar et al. (1994) demonstrate that, in a similar period, there was perceived improvement marked by an increase in admitted bullying, as evidence of more open attitudes, but a decline in reported victims. Young (1994) has shown how students are an important element in driving successful change and Hazler (1994) links this drive to a collective will to foster a good work environment. Our evidence is that in those schools where there is a student and staff awareness of the problem, and where there is determination to bring about changed attitudes, anti-bullying policies are more than a statement on the classroom wall but are a way of life for all members of the community.

# 4 SCHOOL CULTURE

## Introduction

There is no easy way to overcome the subjectivity of students' views of school life which appear to be based on a combination of hearsay, folklore and personal experience re-interpreted over time. When asked to describe five good things about their school experience, the 115 interviewees presented a random selection of features analysed in Table 4.1. These reveal both the range of criteria for 'good schools' and the appreciation by students of friendship, especially in early adolescence, and of teachers at the time when examination demands increase. Whilst these individual features can be classified as relating to peer relationships, staff relationships, work and activities, the interviewees also frequently referred to their association with a good school without a ready ability to determine what made this so – after all, their experience, in most instances, was of one senior school only. One interviewee described the school as 'a good place to be because it is the only chance I get to see my friends and the staff do their best to help you' and to another it is 'a happy school where you do as you are told but they treat you fairly', whilst to a third, 'there are things about the school which aren't good but I wouldn't want to go anywhere else because they do help you to make the most of yourself and I want a good job'. All three comments include assumptions based upon minimal fact but considerable folklore.

Stoll and Fink (1996) demonstrate the link between a positive summative experience in the school and the possibility of school improvement through cooperative attitudes between teachers and pupils in teaching and learning and social interaction. Beare *et al*. (1989) deal at length with managing this school culture to build a structure for school improvement. They outline (1989: 18), a shared value system which develops within close communities and manifests itself in its simplest terms as a 'tribal' way of doing things, although this is a manifestation of deeper value sets. In our survey this was shown in the specific language of place – as in one school

**Table 4.1** Positive features of school life listed by boys and girls ($n = 115$)

| Feature | Year 7 | | Year 8 | | Year 9 | | Year 10 | | Year 11 | | Totals | |
|---|---|---|---|---|---|---|---|---|---|---|---|---|
| | Boys | Girls | Boys | Girls | Boys | Girls | Boys | Girls | Boys | Girls | Boys | Girls |
| Sports | 3 | 0 | 3 | 2 | 5 | 1 | 4 | 2 | 2 | 1 | 17 | 6 |
| Music | | | 1 | 2 | 0 | 2 | | | 1 | 1 | 2 | 5 |
| Activities | 0 | 2 | 1 | 0 | 3 | 3 | 1 | 2 | 3 | 3 | 8 | 10 |
| Work | 2 | 3 | 1 | 3 | 6 | 4 | 6 | 2 | 3 | 2 | 18 | 14 |
| Challenge | 2 | 1 | 0 | 1 | 3 | 1 | 2 | 3 | 0 | 1 | 7 | 7 |
| Buildings | | | 4 | 0 | 1 | 0 | 3 | 3 | 4 | 0 | 12 | 3 |
| Facilities | 0 | 1 | 4 | 0 | 6 | 1 | 4 | 1 | 2 | 1 | 16 | 4 |
| Results | | | | | | | 1 | 0 | | | 1 | 0 |
| Anti-bullying | 1 | 0 | 2 | 1 | 0 | 1 | 2 | 0 | | | 5 | 2 |
| Dress code | | | | | 1 | 2 | | | | | 1 | 2 |
| Fairness | 0 | 1 | | | 2 | 0 | 2 | 6 | 2 | 1 | 6 | 7 |
| Friends | 4 | 3 | 6 | 4 | 9 | 13 | 7 | 9 | 5 | 4 | 31 | 33 |
| Sociability | 0 | 2 | 1 | 2 | 4 | 3 | 2 | 5 | 4 | 4 | 11 | 16 |
| Relationships | 1 | 2 | 1 | 2 | 1 | 1 | 1 | 1 | 2 | 5 | 6 | 11 |
| Teachers | 2 | 3 | 6 | 4 | 4 | 4 | 8 | 6 | 3 | 2 | 23 | 19 |
| Treatment | 0 | 1 | | | 2 | 1 | 1 | 4 | 3 | 1 | 6 | 7 |

where there were references to 'the boys' yard' and 'the top corridor rooms' (a collective noun really intended to imply the anticipated response to disciplinary matters from the senior management staff who occupy these rooms); or of people – 'the counsellor, Mrs X, who is always ready to listen', contrasted with 'Mr Y as the hardest of the year heads'. The location and practice of breaktime smoking, the use of flour and water in unofficial birthday rituals and common understanding of what will happen in the event of a bullying incident, all contribute to the student view of culture. Dalin (1993) shows how external influences such as rapid technological change affect the expectations of pupils and whilst the manifestation of culture may change, for example in the norms of acceptable language imported from television, the school remains as a stable force underpinning essential values such as truth, responsibility and tolerance. The promotion of the set of basic values is fundamental to the successful introduction of any policies concerned with social interaction. Changing culture may require a re-examination of the value system of the organization. In the words of one headteacher, 'we needed to look afresh at what we wanted the young people to remember as their school experience because it will affect them for life'.

The database of evidence suggests that interviewees from the same school recognize the same features of culture to a greater or lesser extent.

One way of measuring this is to attempt to establish an index based upon elements of the evidence given by interviewees. Where all interviewees give evidence of a set of positive shared values of social behaviour in the school an index of 1 is achieved, where only half recognize this the index would be 0.5. By applying this simple analytical tool to the 13 schools for which full interview data is available the lowest index (0.4) occurs in one school, one school achieves each of 0.5, and 0.6 respectively, four schools have an index of 0.7, 5 of 0.8 and one of 0.9. From this it could be suggested that about half of schools have a highly developed shared value system. Comparison with the evidence of anti-bullying policy development indicates the link between positive culture and action to achieve that culture with five of the six highest scoring schools also providing evidence of student knowledge of anti-bullying policies with an index of 0.8 or better. The lowest scoring school for shared values is also the school with the lowest index for evidence of known anti-bullying policies. It is possible that this is just coincidence but the link between a positive social climate and awareness of policy appears strong.

Martin and Meyerson (1988) writing about change in organizations suggest that culture is a complex pattern of meanings, values and behaviours – deeper than the practices which pertain from time to time. However, these may be shown in different ways.

---

**Reflection**    How is the culture manifest in an organization known to you? Is it possible to assess the importance of culture in giving the organization an identity?

---

The culture may be an integrating mechanism as seen in one school where the detailed and whole-school anti-bullying policy is related to the behaviour ethos as a whole, or a differentiation mechanism reflected in the variety of valid anti-bullying policies practised from year to year within an overall minimalist policy framework in another school. Both of these use cultural modification from a centralist, school, position but in some schools there is a loose association of policies worked out in response to the needs of groups and individuals without any overarching policy. This offers an ambiguity which allows varying cultures to develop within groups. This is seen in the data from several schools where there is a conflict between the senior staff view of policy existence, staff interpretation of policies and the resultant student experience. The environment within which students experience culture can be analysed in terms of social interaction, and of behaviour within the teaching and learning context.

## Social interaction

The playground is the most significant meeting area for social interaction in most schools. Blatchford (1993) has stressed the importance of the management of the environment, particularly for younger pupils, to over-come physical situations such as areas hidden from staff view, and the use of positive structured play opportunities to avoid opportunities for secre-tive bullying behaviour. Higgins (1994), again in a primary school context, has shown how environmental change is needed to overcome the inci-dence of bullying related to boredom, overcrowding and marginalization within the playground areas. For some of the interviewees in the current project playground contact, or indeed, exclusion, is an extension of a living hell. One girl spoke of

> going out into the playground because there is no possibility of stay-ing in school only to find that you are caught by the group who have got it in for you and that there is no going away from the taunting . . . I would tell my parents but they already have enough worry and there is very little they can do to get help because the staff only say that I should not take any notice of it.

For another:

> there are separate yards for boys and girls and I don't think that that is fair when we get moved off the boys' yard because some of my clos-est friends are boys and I think it is important to mix . . . people smoke round the back of school and I hate walking round there because loads of big gangs hang around there.

Students are not without their own ideas for improving their social environment especially at lunch-time when one suggests that:

> maybe we could have some lunch-time activities, we have the com-puter club but I don't think that's enough . . . maybe we could also have a games room for cards and other games, also we could maybe get some picnic benches as long as we keep the litter down by putting bins by the side of the benches . . . maybe we could have proper foot-ball and basketball matches in the hall and even use a portable snooker table . . . we could also get some football goals for use at lunch-time.

Other research has shown the extent to which bullies, victims and not-involved students interact with each other. For example, Boulton (1994) records observations of a group of 8–10-year-old boys in the playground situation and defines participation in rule games, social contact or loner behaviour. He found that bullies were twice as likely as victims to be involved in rule games, but that victims were almost twice as likely to be involved in social contact and four times as likely to be loners. Whilst our investigation was with much older students their comments indicate the continuing existence of the three types of social interaction during unstructured leisure time. The development of successful policies for social interaction depends upon recognition of changing student grouping arrangements in a variety of situations – the playground, in class, in the corridors on the way to assembly, and so on. The behaviour pattern which emerges in each situation appears to spring from pupil perception of the behaviour which will be tolerated in the area, the degree of staff supervision and the particular culture associated with the area. One girl commented that:

> there are some girls who when they are moving about the classroom are butter-wouldn't-melt-in-my-mouth sorts and the teachers think that they are great, but when they are in the girls loo with no staff about they change . . . they are horrible, mean and try to get money from me . . . and I know that I can't get help because the rule there is that you don't grass.

Comparison of self-esteem indicators with the incidence of bully or victim experience suggests that up to 10 per cent of all students lack confidence in coping with a range of social situations. Of the 4600 respondents, 6 per cent consider that they are rarely or never fun to be with, 10 per cent are rarely or never popular with their group, 20 per cent feel that their life within school is mostly or always tough and 19 per cent mostly or always feel that they have a low opinion of themselves. Against this background, the 24 per cent who believe that they are often or frequently teased, and the 8 per cent who admit to often or frequently physically hurting others, could be considered to be part of some or all of these groups. Student reaction endorses this view with the complexity of self-confidence, self-esteem and reactive behaviour reflected in the following comment:

> some of my friends in other years or classes stick up for me if someone is being horrible to me . . . most of my friends haven't got the guts to stick up for themselves so I (or some people who can) end up doing it for them . . . I don't think it's fair that a person should be made to do something they don't want to, e.g. in PE or read something out or do a play in front of the whole class.

Interaction also takes place in movement about the school between lessons and of the questionnaire respondents 339 boys (17 per cent) and 366 girls (21 per cent) report being recently physically bullied at that time. The opportunity for name-calling and teasing is reflected in the reported incidents by a much greater number of 707 boys (38 per cent) and 759 girls (44 per cent). For these people the opportunity for name-calling is the most significant feature. One comments:

I know someone who was beaten up by a girl in our year, told the police and the girl that bullied her got suspended for one week and now she teases her and calls her names when she sees her in the corridor.

Another, a boy interviewee, spoke of

the need to get away from others in the corridor because of the pushing and shoving so that what looks accidental can be an opportunity for saying hurtful things and harming you when gangs get together.

This collective noun is frequently used and suggests that anti-bullying policies have to address group as well as individual behaviour.

## Gangs

All three sources of evidence refer to the existence of gangs as part of the social culture of the school. Just under 60 per cent of the respondents acknowledge the existence of gangs in the school and 21 per cent say that they belong to gangs of one sort or another. There is no difference between male and female responses, but there is an increase in admitted gang membership from 15 per cent in Year 7 to 24 per cent in Year 10. However, the maturation factor appears to operate at that stage and there is a fall to 21 per cent in Year 11. Whilst the gangs may operate as collective bullying forces within the school they also appear to be linked to external gangs with an 'extended family of those who used to attend the school and are now loose in the community'. The impact of the local group as a factor in school behaviour patterns is frequently publicly suppressed but may still affect individuals who are manipulated by external, and older colleagues (Van Reenan 1992). Student perceptions of gang activity are shown in the comments that 'it depends on which pupils are around – most are OK but we get the odd older girl gang who think that they rule the school and whatever they say goes', 'groups try and pressure you into trying things like cigarettes, drugs and so on . . .' and

amongst the year I know of a number of girl groups or gangs consisting of about six to eight girls, and between the different groups there is trouble about boy friends, clothes, looks, where you're seen and so on . . . if this could be sorted out then I would feel a lot more comfortable at school.

For Jason, a Year 8 pupil who could find no good things about school, groups have

picked on me and called me names leaving me miserable, upset and taking days off school because I could not cope, it needs staff to do something and they should be backed up by police action to give these others a hard time.

The extension into the community is shown in the interview with Kathryn, a Year 10 pupil, who spoke of the tension between gangs from two rival schools and consequent fights based on misplaced loyalty. The effect of this is shown in the account by Jenny, in Year 11, of the personal fear caused by a group of older girls who tracked her down after school and then continued to taunt her 'as a means of securing compliance with protection . . . at a price'.

Once again, students are able to give their own views of successful strategies for managing problems. All these imply knowledge of cultural norms and processes in the school. Rachel, in Year 9, suggests that

> groups of friends bicker and argue but it is usually short term . . . it would be a good idea if these groups of friends are mixed up so that they work with and get to know other pupils outside their usual friendship groups.

Richard, in the same year, praises the staff knowledge of the student grapevine so that

> when a big fight between gangs was planned for after school, off the premises, the head and staff patrolled the immediate area to disperse the students and ensure that the flashpoint was defused.

The exclusion of unwanted gang members is detailed by Mark in year 8 who

> would like to see the school sealed off from outside with only one gate allowing access through a key card system . . . this would stop trespassers who mainly hang about the gates coming on to school grounds and starting trouble with the existing pupils.

All these ideas conform with those offered as a result of other research. Holmes (1995) considers that the maturation process is more difficult now than in former years and that further consideration needs to be given to enhancing student understanding of group behaviours and peer pressure.

---

**Reflection**   What are the factors which may contribute to Holmes' assertion that maturation is now a more difficult process? How can schools change the culture of the gang?

It is unlikely that the gangs described above are so closely integrated or controlled as to match those urban gangs with violently enforced codes of behaviour described by Berndt (1992). Interviewees refer to the groups as 'just a gang of my mates' or 'part of the crowd of people who stay together' but it is the collective power of the group which intimidates the isolate and loner and which leads 16 per cent of males and 23 per cent of females to mostly or always give in under pressure. Humphrey and Baker (1994) have developed a programme of training for urban gangs based upon appreciation of the victim situation, knowledge of cultural diversity, conflict resolution and personal and community responsibilities. A similar programme, developed by the Police Research Group (Pitts and Smith 1996), has been successful in two tightly defined urban areas in securing some reduction in victimization for all except Bengali racial groups. The topics outlined in these programmes are mirrored in the personal and social education syllabuses of some of the sample schools illustrated in Chapter 5.

## Classroom culture

The influence of gangs is less obvious in classroom situations but comments from interviewees show how they can still act to intimidate. The cause of problems within the classroom situation appears twofold – the assumption by students that their work effort must be made without it being obvious to peers and that weaker members of staff are an easy prey for those students who want to show themselves as being 'hard'.

One girl records that another threw a table at her because of her refusal to be distracted during a German lesson; another says that she 'is good at writing poems so people say she is a swot'. Two Year 11 boys spoke of the dilemma of completing work without letting others in the class know that they were making any effort and their hope that teachers would comply with their 'no fuss' needs. But not all disagreement is about achievement and less than positive behavioural norms are developed under peer pressure. These include name-calling in work situations, abusive language, sexual and racist innuendo, and group behaviours including 'having a laugh at the teacher's expense', 'taking property just to tease' and 'being shut out of the work group'. The fudged boundaries perceived by students between misbehaviour and bullying are clear in this evaluation of classroom life but the accepted responsibility by students indicates that they may well bully teachers as well as peers.

The role of the teacher is also considered by students to be significant in managing anti-social behaviour. Nicci, a Year 7 girl, refers to the importance of teachers in maintaining discipline and in keeping the whole class working; David, a Year 11 boy, is more selective in his view that teachers are the most important control mechanism and that bullying may develop where they are less vigilant or where they 'actually support the bullies by failing to intervene in the hope that the problem will go away'. Again, there is evidence that the staff of some schools have a more highly developed and shared set of expectations of students. Pupils were questioned in the interviews about classroom management and an index based on the proportion of responses indicating consistent teacher control was developed. This showed a range from 0.4 (three schools), 0.6 (five schools), 0.8 (two schools), 0.9 (one school) and 1.0 (two schools). Again, the school with the least developed anti-bullying policies is included in the lowest scoring group, whilst both the schools with the highest score have provided evidence of whole staff approaches to behaviour management. The link between positive culture, high expectations and clear codes of work and behaviour in the highly rated schools is not one of chance and schools seeking to improve overall clearly need to consider attitudes to problems, including bullying (Reid et al. 1987). Within the classroom this appears to require that there is effective control of student interaction in three ways.

First, the organization of working groups requires care in managing pupil interaction to avoid disharmony. One respondent comments that 'it is important that all the staff should watch the way in which groups are organized and work together' and this accords with the analysis of Cowie and Sharp (1994) that working in cooperative groups enhances the development of corporate action against prejudice. The risk is that any marginalization could be even more marked than in whole-class teaching situations; as one boy comments, 'a lot of people I work with cause trouble for me because they get jealous of my good work and have a go at me . . . this gets me down and puts me off doing any further good work'. The advantage is reflected in the interview comment of Tracey, a Year 8 girl, that 'working together means that we sort problems out between ourselves alongside our work'. Second, staff control of language used between pupils whilst involved in the work situation also appears to be important in ensuring shared values by students. One respondent says that 'this school is bad for the amount of abuse pupils receive from one another and teachers are not always supportive enough'. The third element of classroom management which respondents and interviewees identify is the belief in fairness and consistency in dealing with all situations. This is shown in the comment that 'if the bully is a student who is well liked and popular, teachers would not take it quite as seriously as if I were talking about a well-known troublemaker' and 'teachers seem sometimes to be blind to what is going on in their lessons – either that or they are just ignoring it'. Students are also aware of the need for continuing supervision – to one, 'although the teachers were very helpful when I had trouble they ought to realize that the situation would require help for a longer period to stop the trouble under the surface'.

In some way, over 30 per cent of those who were interviewed felt that teachers did not take complaints seriously and 15 per cent comment on aspects of bullying behaviour by the staff such as 'sometimes the teachers bully you without you knowing', 'the teachers talk to you in a way which makes you feel worse' and 'the teachers only hear those things they want to hear because they have already decided that they do not like you'. At the same time, we should note that there were many positive comments on the way in which teachers acted including 'most of the teachers are very understanding and treat people fairly . . . if somebody has done anything wrong they get a fair punishment' and 'the teachers are ready to listen to you – mostly – and they have helped without making things worse'. The efficacy of intervention is a topic we shall return to in Chapter 6.

## Perceptions of school culture

The involvement of pupils in the management of their own social inter-action has been an important feature of the establishment of a supportive environment in some schools. In one of the schools surveyed, students have identified those areas of the school where there are potential prob-lems as part of the work of the students' council. The senior management team have then linked supervisory duties to the establishment of particu-lar watch in those areas where there has been difficulty. In another, part of the English curriculum looks at the language and norms of the playground and then uses opportunities in drama to explore the ideas which students bring forward for working out conflict. There are however, indications that the staff of schools do not always exert the same pressures for positive social behaviour and that some social interaction is inhibited by student misunderstanding of the aims and values of the school.

School culture is a nebulous concept embracing all elements of the life of students and staff within the structure and organization which makes each school unique. Hargreaves (1995) details the culture of schools as a combination of social control through structures and rules, and social cohesion which is achieved through the stimulation of creativity and shared values. Schools which are high in control offer procedures when dealing with anti-bullying based upon 'a succession of punishments', 'immediate suspension until the difficulties are resolved' and 'the require-ment that the bully should recognize his or her debt to the victim'. Those which are high in cohesion appear to be more 'concerned to develop a policy which the youngsters want to follow', to 'base relationships in the school on a shared understanding of respect' and to 'offer both sides in any dispute the opportunity to find a way forward'. There are some schools in our sample which have high control and cohesion approaches leading to what Hargreaves calls a 'hothouse' approach in which the flexibility demanded of social cohesion is constrained by the need to act within the control mechanisms – reflected in the comment of one Year 11 student that 'the school is strongly anti-bullying and we understand why this is but some of the action taken against bullies is unfair because staff act without understanding each situation'. In another school, a girl comments that 'teachers, parents and others should hear both sides of the argument, not just the victim's side and decide on fair punishments not immediate suspension as this makes the situation even worse'. Two of the sample schools appear to have low control and low cohesion marked by a variety of practice and a degree of confusion amongst students and staff about the nature of policy and practice reflected in the view that 'there is a policy but I don't know what it is because all the teachers act differently except to tell you that it is wrong to bully others'. Hargreaves offers a fifth situation, that where effectiveness is maintained because of a combination of optimal control with optimal cohesion. This is evident in one of the schools where students comment that

> this is a good school because we know what we can and can't do . . . there is a procedure when people fall out and teachers always separate them and continue as normally as possible until they are able to sit down with both parties and sort through the problem . . . the aim is to work it out with both and to involve parents and friends if it helps the situation . . . but it is not always the same when it comes to punishment because the blame is not always the same.

A culture which allows creativity within a framework of control clearly establishes principles but allows for variation in practice to meet the needs of the situation.

Morgan (1986) questions the validity of the cultural metaphor and sees a tension between the establishment of a shared view of the organization in terms of 'this is a friendly school with good relationships between students and staff' and the reality of individual perception where a student within the school comments, 'I hate it here and just long to get away because I don't fit'. Sisken (1994) considers the importance of subcultures which develop amongst the staff and the students. In one of the schools considered in detail respondents have been quick to recognize that

> there are some staff who remind you of the anti-bullying policy as part of what we do in form periods and who really stand by it but other teachers don't think it is so important and they either don't do anything or they tell you to grow up and things will change.

Convincing staff of the need for some cultural change was at the heart of the evolution of successful anti-bullying policies in the schools which were investigated. Mulhern (1994) in an attempt to reduce violent behaviour in groups of adolescents details the significance of self-esteem, personal and social responsibility and confidence in non-violent problem solving approaches as a framework for change upon which agreed shared practice can be based. Thompson *et al.* (1994a) offer the principles of integration of anti-bullying attitudes with whole-school behaviour policies, stress on equal opportunities policies and the involvement of all staff and support agencies in the development of policy as essential starting points. Comment from staff in two of the schools suggests that there is some reluctance by staff 'to appear to go soft on bullies' and this may inhibit positive action.

---

**Reflection**   What do you see as the advantages and disadvantages of a specific anti-bullying policy? Is it affected by the cultural context of the school?

---

## Towards policy development

Our investigation has shown that schools are at differing starting points in developing their own policies. This is because of the varying value placed upon anti-bullying amongst the priorities for consideration. One head commented that 'we are only really thinking about it because parents are asking but it is not a problem', whilst another said that 'it is a fundamental belief that every child has an equal right to happiness and the freedom to gain as much as possible from school and that is our starting point'. Against this there is also evidence of a real fear amongst the senior managers of some schools that 'whilst there is always some bullying within schools we don't want to make too much of developing a policy because we would not want parents of potential students to be put off by the thought that we had a problem'. On the other hand, several of the schools in the investigation have involved parents and pupils in the development of a policy with maximum local publicity to allow open discussion of issues. This is, in itself, a reflection of the open and closed systems which operate between the schools and its environment.

The most frequently given reason for change is that policies were developed as a result of a wish to bring about consistent practice and to meet national pressures arising from media attention. Overall though, interview evidence suggests that policy creation has arisen from a desire to 'establish decent behaviour as the norm in schools' and to help 'to develop a rounded person within a pleasant constructive atmosphere'. However, there is also evidence that whilst there may be a widespread ownership of the policy with staff feeling that they have made a worthwhile contribution to the discussion, there is also a need for either a group of staff or an individual to maintain the momentum if cultural change is to become embedded in the life of the school. The production of policies alone is not a sufficient spur to cultural change. Stoll and Fink (1996) in their assessment of the successful management of change within a Canadian school district stress the importance of shared goals, shared responsibility, collegial approaches, continuous improvement, risk-taking, mutual respect and support in making change work. Our evidence is that some schools have introduced policies as a peripheral activity whilst fundamental change may be necessary.

# ⑤ SCHOOL POLICIES

## Introduction

In Chapter 4 we observed how members of a school who share the same caring values can produce a supportive culture which provides security for all. Moreover, our evidence suggested a strong link between a positive social climate and the effectiveness of anti-bullying policies. This chapter will explore how far the establishment of such policies can contribute to this kind of school ethos. It will examine how and when policies were established, the rationale and motivation behind them, the detail involved, the curriculum implications, the pastoral context, the school culture, the publicizing and communication of practice, and the use of monitoring and evaluation.

## Background

Arora and Thompson (1987) stress the importance of whole-school anti-bullying policies. These include formalized documents, recurrent themes in pastoral and social education (PSE), appropriate curriculum materials, and support structures such as reporting, self-help and counselling procedures. Any school's policy will be unique to suit its particular circumstances but it usually consists of publicly written intentions and practical applications of strategies to deal with bullying behaviour and its consequences. The rationale for having such a policy, apart from satisfying the increasing expectations that all schools should have them, is usually threefold. A policy makes clear to everyone in the school community what the school is doing about bullying and why; it communicates clearly that bullying is not tolerated; and it can be used to monitor progress. The people involved in policymaking varies from school to school but ideally as many representative groups as possible are included such as teachers, governors, students, parents, caretakers, lunch-time supervisors, and administrative and ancillary staff. The process of discussion and awareness raising in itself is often seen as important as the written policy.

All except five of the schools surveyed have anti-bullying policies which are either written separately or as part of other written policies such as behaviour, pastoral or equal opportunities policies. Two of these policies are not written down although they are practised and known and one is written for staff only. Of the 18 policies sent to us, half are short documents concentrating on a school definition of bullying with a summary of how it is manifested and their procedures for dealing with it. The Greensward High School policy, shown below, was developed after whole-school discussion. The other half of the written policies are more detailed, covering organization and administration, detailed procedures, responsibilities of staff, symptoms and effects of bullying, specific strategies and plans for

---

**Greensward High School anti-bullying policy**

*Aim:* 'To emphasize that bullying, both verbal and physical will not be tolerated.'

A student needs a secure, happy and friendly environment in order to learn effectively.
Bullying is the wilful conscious desire to physically or emotionally hurt another person or to put her or him under stress.
Bullying can be in a variety of forms: physical; verbal; extortion; exclusion from groups; spreading malicious gossip; threatening gestures; theft of property; and sexual and racial harassment.

Bullying will be dealt with by:
- making students aware of what bullying involves
- reminding students of their rights and responsibilities
- making sure that students know how to seek support if their rights are being violated
- encouraging students to help and respect each other
- encouraging students to talk about any problems they are experiencing
- asking parents to discuss any problems they know or suspect their child is having
- applying fair, firm and consistent sanctions
- discussing problems and incidents fully with all concerned
- carefully monitoring any incidents of bullying.

IN CASES OF SEVERE OR PERSISTENT BULLYING THE GOVERNORS RESERVE THE RIGHT TO EXCLUDE THE STUDENT/STUDENTS CONCERNED

the future. These longer policies are put in staff and student handbooks and are available for parents. They expect all personnel to take action and specifically outlines strategies to be used by staff such as the policy for Greylands High School.

---

**Greylands High School anti-bullying policy**

We seek to create a climate in school whereby bullying behaviours are not accepted by any member of the school community.
Our policy aims to use all students, staff and parents to work towards the elimination of any form of bullying.

We aim to:
Use all staff, parents and students to prevent and not just control bullying.
Use the curriculum as a means of raising awareness of the school's expectations.
Give help and ongoing support to victims.
Help and give support to bullies to change their behaviour.
Inform parents/carers of the repetition of any unacceptable behaviour.
Encourage pupils to reject anti-social behaviour.
Seek the involvement of outside professional agencies if and where necessary.

We have an expectation of parents that they should be supportive in the process of eliminating any form of bullying.

'A BULLY IS A PERSON WHO REGULARLY CAUSES SUFFERING TO OTHERS BY ANY WORD OR DEED'

---

**Greylands High School anti-bullying staff policy**

| | |
|---|---|
| BE AVAILABLE | Whoever is approached must arrange a time to discuss the problem and ensure that the child is seen before the end of the day. |
| INVESTIGATE | Take pupil/s to a quiet secure location and interview. |
| RECORD | Obtain a written record of events from (a) the victim (b) the suspected bully (c) any witness |
| RESPOND | Make the bully aware that future problems will lead to the involvement of their parents. |

|               | Ask the victim if his/her parents have been informed. (It may be necessary to send a letter to the parents of both parties). |
|---|---|
|               | Inform form teacher and year tutor of victim and bully and involve when necessary the member of the SMT with responsibility for discipline. |
| REVIEW        | Review the situation in a purposeful manner and reassure pupils. |
| PROTECTION    | Problems outside the school gates can prove difficult as they are not our responsibility but the member of staff involved should take the necessary steps to ensure the safe return home of the victim. |

Some policies, such as the ones reproduced here, are often in the form of leaflets to be distributed to all school personnel and the public. The shorter policies, as well as appearing in handbooks and leaflets, are usually made into posters and displayed around the schools as in the case of Northings High School which is directed towards the students.

---

**Northings High School**

**Our school does not accept bullying in any form. Remember that!**

**Your rights**    As a member of Northings School you have the right:
- to live your life in peace and safety
- get on with your work
- to be an individual and be proud of being different
- not to be bullied
- to say 'no' firmly to anything you think is wrong
- to protect yourself by ignoring others and walking away
- to TELL a member of staff if someone is making you unhappy

**Your responsibilities**    Our school expects you:
- not to put up with any form of bullying
- to help to stop others bullying
- not to be afraid to report bullying in any form – you will be supported
- not to keep bullies' secrets – it might suggest you are supporting the bully
- not to put up with bullies in your group of friends
- to support other pupils who are bullied

---

## Establishing policies

A small number of schools established their written policies as long ago as 1990 but the majority have been formed over the last few years. Their origins reflect the management culture of each school and the evidence accords with much of the work on change in education explored by Fullan (1991). The rationale may have been philosophical as 'part of a general framework of behaviour and conduct with positive pupil–teacher relationships and by pupil awareness that all staff will help' or because 'bullying is a denial of equal opportunity for all pupils as a fundamental moral principle'. At the other extreme it may have been a pragmatic reaction to 'national pressures and the impending Ofsted inspection'.

Thirteen schools gave specific reasons for developing their policies with nine being formed as a response to outside forces such as national pressures, media publicity and parental influence. Three of these felt an anti-bullying policy was 'fundamental' in encouraging recruitment. According to one headteacher, 'parental choice demands it'. Another three schools developed policies as a direct response to forthcoming Ofsted inspections and the need to prepare the necessary documents. In one of these 'the profile was raised as a result of media pressure and the written document was precipitated by the impending Ofsted inspection which caused the school to evaluate what it was doing'.

Some schools, on the other hand, saw a need for anti-bullying work to address particular problems in school which were being either caused or exacerbated by bullying behaviour. Research has highlighted close links between bullying, school refusal, disruptive behaviour, anxiety and inhibition (Chazan et al. 1994) and also between bullying, boredom and under-achievement (Gleeson 1994). The impact of bullying on students' learning is demonstrated by Hazler (1994) who advocates a proactive stance to prevent a climate that allows bullying and harassment to flourish. A link had already been established by Olweus (1991) between the effect of school based anti-bullying work and the improvement in other forms of anti-social behaviour.

Four schools initiated policies as a response to problems arising from incidents of bullying and its effect on teaching and learning. One of these was motivated by an inset day on 'Success in Lessons' to develop a 'Code of Conduct' linked with proactive and assertive discipline rather than adopting an anti-bullying policy as such. It was felt by the deputy head-teacher that, 'improved behaviour was important to lessons and improved learning so that's why anti-bullying is only part of school policy'. Another school's anti-bullying initiative 'arose out of the Keele [Partnership] pupil attitude surveys in 1994 . . . in the parents' survey 13 per cent reported that bullying was a problem'. The school began a planning cycle to improve the situation and the anti-bullying policy became part of what the deputy headteacher referred to as 'a whole-school policy towards the personal security and happiness of students'.

Students themselves raised the issue in some schools. La Fontaine (1991) provides evidence that young people's descriptions of bullying challenge those of adults. They understand bullying in terms of the impact on them, define a wider range of behaviour as bullying and they want it stopped. A group of students in one school perceived the need to do something about bullying and enlisted the support of the school counsellor, the local police and two campaigning charities to raise awareness primarily with students in a whole-school day workshop with representatives from other town schools. It led to a whole-school anti-bullying policy initiated by students.

For most schools, however, anti-bullying policies were staff-led rather than student led. There is no doubt that teachers are aware of the nature and incidence of the physical and verbal bullying in their classrooms as is shown in survey material in the Elton report (see page 1). The policy may have been evolved by a limited group of staff or following general discussion. At one extreme a tutor commented, 'I vaguely recall a pile of papers in my pigeon hole' whilst at the other end of the spectrum 'the policy evolved as a result of staff discussion which was then considered by the senior management team who made proposals which were refined by the pastoral committee and thence to the governors at a time when the profile was raised by media pressure which caused the school to evaluate procedures'. It appears that those schools which tended towards the latter pattern have become more successful as judged by the consistency of staff and pupil understanding of what the policy is. In the school from which the first comment came there is mention of an element of staff bullying and pupils refer to the 'shouting by staff' in dealing with problems.

In one school, whilst there is evidence that bullying is dealt with seriously there is no written policy. In another, there is reference to the 'strong and continuing influence of the pastoral deputy head and the school counsellor giving a dynamic lead and they will not be deflected but they have given middle management staff their heads as leaders of the programme'. That is not to say that the first school is unsuccessful in its anti-bullying stance because 'whilst there is no formal policy there are well-established practices known to all staff'. Rather, policies within the second school are perceived to be more effective because known plans and procedures are shared by all staff and of the 13 pupils interviewed, 10 commended the school for the way in which staff dealt with problems.

In 15 of the Keele Partnership study schools, the initiator was the headteacher or a member of the senior management or pastoral team, although at least two of these have subsequently encouraged a bottom-up approach with students and classroom teachers taking a strong lead. Stone (1995) demonstrates by comparing three school initiatives that a bottom-up ownership of change approach does most to raise expectations. In the school where the students initiated the policy the support and encouragement of their teachers was crucial for further development. The headteacher said, 'the overall influence in recent years has been the part played by staff below senior management level'. Another school has a similar approach, 'the senior management team are not involved in order to avoid top-down development'.

Working parties have been popular ways of developing policy in this way. At least eight schools have such groups of usually between four and eight members to write draft policies for discussion by the rest of the staff before finalization. Twelve of the schools with policies have involved all staff to some extent. Nine schools worked with parents, five schools specifically involved students from school councils, and at least one received an input from lunch-time supervisors. It appears that those schools with a high involvement of a cross-section of school personnel in the policy development were more likely to create a common ownership of it, as judged by the consistency of staff and student understanding of the basic ideas in their policy. In schools where policies were presented to staff 'without consultation and not enough student input' there was a vague, inconsistent and often confused response. One head of year commented, 'the policy has no shared definitions, dinner supervisors are not included and the policy is not owned by enough people to effect the culture'. Seven schools appear to have policies which are not fully understood by the whole staff for this reason and are having a minimum impact. In four of the latter schools, there is evidence that the initial reasons for introducing the policies also influenced how they were perceived by staff. They were instigated primarily as a result of external pressure, such as Ofsted or student recruitment rather than by a need perceived from within the school.

Where there is not a sense of whole-school ownership of anti-bullying policies, there appears to be less evidence of shared positive values. The year head quoted in the paragraph above felt there was:

> a philosophical chasm especially with regard to no blame policies . . . the anti-bullying policy was presented without consultation . . . the pupil input was not enough, and the school council did not see themselves as part of the process . . . the group culture of the dinner women is too exclusive and they were not involved in talking with the staff.

Yet in the same school the headteacher stated that the policy, 'evolved from the school council' and the deputy headteacher believes 'there is a commitment to take the no blame policy seriously'.

At least twelve schools where teachers were interviewed seem to have values which are shared by the majority of staff although in several schools these are not shared by parents. The qualities which are valued highly by these schools include respectful relationships, cooperation, consideration to others, tolerance, non-intimidation, relaxed orderliness, safety and no fear for students, self-responsibility, 'rounded persons', no blame approaches and a friendly ethos. It seems that even when there is a widespread ownership of a policy there is also a need for a group of staff or an individual to maintain the momentum lest the priority be overtaken by more pressing concerns amongst staff. As Wallace (1991) shows, too many objectives may result in loss of drive. In one school 'there is no written policy in existence . . . a working party was set up three or four years ago with interested staff but following the retirement of the deputy at that time there is need for a new start'. In another the headteacher pointed out that the policy was in its infancy when he arrived and acknowledged 'the dynamic lead by the school counsellor has been crucial – she will not be deflected!'

Although about half of the schools exhibited a strong sense of sharing the kinds of values listed above not all showed consistency in putting them into practice. One senior teacher felt the anti-bullying policy of his school fitted into the overall pastoral policy. 'The ethos is friendly and pupils and staff are sensitized to a great many issues.' However, in the same school, a female teacher pointed out that 'sexual innuendo and misplaced humour of staff is a problem here and some staff believe bullying is normal'. This observation echoes Olweus (1978) who raises the question of whether staff think bullying is part of the normal life of the school. There are a number of studies (Ziegler and Rosenstein-Manner 1991; Pervin and Turner 1994) which reflect the underestimation by teachers of bullying compared with self and peer reports by students. Personnel from ten of the responding schools commented on a need for more consistency and in three it was pointed out that staff are bullies themselves, either towards each other or to the students. In one school, it was claimed that: 'There is a culture of bullying between some senior management team members and staff which is passed on to children.' In another, there is 'a somewhat bullying atmosphere in the school – staff, especially women staff, suffer from bullying by male colleagues'.

A common theme in comments from staff who wish to improve the situations in schools where there is this kind of inconsistent approach is the need for induction and training for staff in bullying issues. This for many schools was the first step towards a formal policy. Although the most common starting point is the setting up of an anti-bullying working party, there are a number of others including:

- conducting surveys of students to find out the extent and nature of the problem;
- having assemblies on the theme of bullying;
- organizing a whole school day workshop for students on bullying;
- having a bullying-awareness day, week or month;
- students making anti-bullying posters to be displayed around the school;
- and hiring a theatre group to perform a play on bullying.

## Determining the detail

The detail of a written policy is mostly determined by the reasons for having the policy and the practical needs for a school embarking upon it. In the schools which sent us their policies the following elements were covered in various degrees:

- a positive statement of ethos and the kind of behaviour expected;
- a clear definition of bullying as agreed by the whole school;
- an explanation of how bullying behaviour is manifested and by whom;
- procedures for dealing with bullying to be taken by staff, students bullied and their parents;
- support available for recipients and perpetrators of bullying;
- training implications for staff;
- financing the policy;
- the means of monitoring, review and promotion of the policy; and
- the people who have been involved in developing it.

The school which started with a whole-school day workshop in 1989 for student discussions continued to develop its policy over a period of six years introducing a number of anti-bullying strategies including a contract signed by all students, a definition of bullying, a peer-counselling service, PSE and other teaching programmes, assemblies, drama and dance productions, surveys, appointing an anti-bullying coordinator and using an award from an international corporation to finance a two-year peer counselling project with two other schools.

Comments from this school and others where policies have been in operation over a period of time can help us to extract a set of considerations for schools contemplating this type of work. The main issue emerging is that as soon as the work is embarked upon expectations are raised. To accommodate this, more time and finance are required for staff and student training. A strong commitment is needed from governors and senior management teams. A named person with time and status to coordinate the policy is also helpful. In particular, time must be allowed for teachers to use the policy as a monitoring tool. Anti-bullying work needs to be a regular agenda item on the meetings of pastoral committee and governing bodies and the policy should ensure that there is an agreed definition of bullying known by all. In one of the schools where this kind of work has not continued the deputy headteacher felt it was because the governors did not want staff to become social workers, and in another the legal obligations falling on teachers in the Children Act was cited as a reason for the discouragement of disclosures.

Evidence suggests that raised expectations do increase disclosures and staff members in two schools interpret this increase as 'the more children are made aware of bullying the more it will occur'. Schools need more time for counselling and guidance to deal with the increase in students asking for help and one school advocates late registration systems to enable more time at the end of the day to act on disclosures. The general consensus is that younger students are more likely to disclose and perhaps this means more work is needed to resolve problems which are being suppressed by the older students. Of the 24 schools who do PSE work on bullying, only seven specifically mention work with Years 10 and 11. Students and teachers in many of the schools pointed out the need for the issue to be kept alive by regular reminders and activities. Teachers in a number of schools point out the difficulties of doing this in terms of time constraints from elsewhere with two headteachers commenting on other priorities including the spread of policy development required for Ofsted inspections. Another school refers to the inhibiting effect of an anti-work ethic causing peer pressure on students not to succeed. One of the form tutors remarked on conformist children not being socially acceptable and 'an intimidating atmosphere with name-calling and anti-work comments'.

## Curriculum implications

In the policy of one school, there is a specific reference to whole-school preventative work that involves the integration of anti-bullying activities into the curriculum with: 'A PSE programme for students to discuss, support, monitor and update the policy and assemblies, drama productions, certain teaching programmes and other means of raising awareness on the subject.'

The schools link their policies into their pastoral and academic curriculum in a variety of ways. Tattum and Herbert (1993) give several examples of schools using their curriculum in this way and point out that, whilst positive steps may be taken in PSE teaching, the pupil still has to attend other classes where fear may be engendered. Twenty-one of the schools which sent documentation refer to proactive work in PSE programmes with fourteen giving exemplar material. However, only ten referred to work in the academic curriculum and only three sent in examples of work from non-PSE subjects in the curriculum. Whereas the former usually focus on various types of awareness-raising and self-esteem work the latter use bullying as a topic to fit into the National Curriculum requirements. One school sent us a copy of a poem written by a student for General Certificate of Secondary Education (GCSE) and which had been published in a national newspaper and an anthology of children's poetry. The same school gave us booklets about bullying by Year 8 students as part of their English Key Stage 3 curriculum. Another provided us with a study guide on bullying for GCSE topic work. Both included poems, narratives, playscripts, accounts of personal experience and the Year 8 booklets allowed for differentiation 'to avoid a sense of failure' with the use of wordsearches and crosswords.

There is evidence to show that some schools in the Keele Partnership recognize that self-esteem contributes to academic achievement as well as improving social skills. Olweus (1978) showed that apart from the physical dangers they are exposed to, victims of bullying may lose their self-esteem and Roland (1980) gave evidence that some victims begin to think that they deserve to be bullied. O'Moore and Hillery (1991) found that bullies had low self-esteem in relation to intellectual and school status and Tattum and Tattum (1992) found that such low self-perceptions are damaging and persist into adulthood. They also showed how bullying affects the bystanders with less aggressive students being drawn in or feeling intimidated.

For a number of schools, it seems to make sense, therefore, to include in their curriculum various strategies for enhancing the self-esteem of its students. Although it can be tempting to see students' minor concerns as unimportant, compared to the pressures of educating them, a number of schools are beginning to see that having high self-esteem is the foundation of effective learning and good relationships. Jones (1994) explains how students use bullying to gain status and power and advocates schools using the curriculum to raise students' self-esteem and for teaching coping strategies. Mulhern (1994) shows how schools can help with esteem building, personal and social responsibility and the development of non-violent problem-solving approaches.

Dymond and Gilmore (1993) list some of the ways in which low self-esteem is manifested in students as underachievement, lack of confidence to think autonomously, being easily led by others, wanting to undermine the self-esteem of others by bullying, having a tendency to become victimized by bullies, having difficulties with forming and maintaining friendships and fear of failing which leads to aggression and/or withdrawal.

They believe that by enabling all students to work on improving self-esteem in the curriculum, schools can help to protect them from being bullied or becoming bullies. They advise schools to enhance self-esteem by valuing student opinion, allowing them real choices, and encouragement in the expression of emotions and feelings in an environment which fosters positive self-image supported by appropriate and genuine praise. The importance attributed to praise and rewards is manifest in much of the document and interview data from schools and two specifically refer to sending letters of praise to parents. However, at least two schools point to the problem of the very able not wanting to be singled out.

> **Reflection** Various forms of discrimination appear to underpin much bullying behaviour. How far does their behaviour reflect the views of society at large? Can we ever break this link?

Listening skills are also focused on by some schools as a means to promote learning. As Dymond and Gilmore point out, students often think listening means sitting still, not fidgeting and developing survival strategies for appearing to listen passively, and then only to the teacher. They point out people often feel that nobody listens to them and class discussions fail when students have difficulty not interrupting each other. Weissglass and Weissglass (1987) focus on the development of active listening skills to promote effective learning. They advocate 'support dyads' whereby people take it in turns to listen and communicate in a more cooperative and less stressful way. 'Articulating your experiences, expressing your feelings to another, and reflecting on the insights you gain are keys to improved learning, teaching and effectiveness.' One school uses this model in the form of co-counselling which is described by Cartwright (1995) as: 'an agreement between two people to take it in turns to listen to each other. When someone really listens to you it is easier to get rid of bad and confusing feelings which stop you thinking clearly.'

Cowie and Sharp (1992) focus on quality circles for involving students in developing solutions to bullying. Circle time is an activity for students to develop listening skills which are active rather than passive and to talk about personal rather than curriculum concerns. It can take place at the beginning and/or end of any lesson and the active listening involved can create a supportive atmosphere. Dymond and Gilmore outline the basic principles of circle time as: 'everyone's position is equal; all the children can see and hear each other; the teacher is part of the circle; the chances of turn-taking and structuring discussion are enhanced; everyone has a responsibility to listen and an opportunity to speak; and listening is non judgmental.' Once established, students see the value of circle times and to have a lasting impact they need to be a regular event. In the same school which uses co-counselling, circle time is used at the beginning of some English lessons once a week with a class of Year 10 boys, many of whom have behavioural and learning difficulties. Also trained peer counsellors from Years 12 and 13 lead circle times in Year 7 tutor groups for ten minutes at the beginning of one morning a week.

Peer counselling, circle time and other listening strategies promote cooperation rather than competition between students. Various studies have demonstrated that schools which inadvertently or purposefully create an overcompetitive ethos can without realizing fail to enable students to work cooperatively towards common goals. One deputy head-teacher referred to 'a problem in creating success acceptability. There can be an ethos around subjects which leads to intimidation.' This contrasts with the more cooperative approaches encouraged in the pastoral system in the school where co-counselling and circle time is used. The head-teacher attributes the loss of 'some of the competitiveness' to 'the change from a house system to a year system. Celebration replaced competition. Celebration of each other's successes replaces winning.' The Elton report found that many problems were associated with a lack of cooperation amongst students. By promoting cooperative attitudes and practices students are helped to acquire social skills which benefit the whole of society.

Documentary evidence from the schools shows a variety of cooperative activities with whole groups engaging in motivating work which enables each member to have an essential role. Work and lesson plans include group book making, poems, stories, brainstorming, group problem-solving and cooperative games. Nine schools refer to work along these lines in subjects like English and drama, four do such work in religious education and two in history, and one each in physical education, dance and science. However, most anti-bullying work seems to be part of PSE programmes which centre on assertiveness and coping strategies, friend-ships and relationships, bullying and aggression, listening and coun-selling skills, and whole-school contracts. Interview data suggest one reason for concentrating this work in PSE is that heads of departments see the issue as primarily a pastoral one. One head of department believed there was a 'lack of confidence in untrained staff to deliver work in this area'. The 'ethos of intimidation' in some subjects referred to by the deputy headteacher in the paragraph above may also account for a preference for work to be done in the pastoral context.

The PSE programmes in eleven of the schools are cyclical to develop the discussion as the students become more mature. In some schools staff with specialist skills develop materials whilst in others they are prepared annu-ally by year teams . All schools use visiting speakers to some extent includ-ing Kidscape, the police and local social workers and thirteen mention sponsored video and role-play materials. Tutorial work is used to approach these issues and in half the schools surveyed this extends, or substitutes for PSE teaching. Despite this pastoral work some schools have difficulty in 'getting students to disclose and discuss openly in PSE'. Perhaps there are dangers in having a too prescriptive approach. A tutor in one school pointed to problems caused by their life studies programme which had links with anti-bullying but was 'too prescribed with not enough time to do informal tutor work with a group when it is appropriate to accommodate issues of the moment'.

Quicke (1995) points out in a study observing pupil interaction in a number of classes that there is a need for greater democracy in managing students. Some schools enhance the democratic process by directly involving anti-bullying working groups in the planning of PSE programmes. For example, one school's working party helped devise a Handling Conflict course for its Year 7 social education programme. It also produced a leaflet and publicizes itself in school bulletins. Another school's group worked alongside its local Health Promotion Unit to design and operate a 100 per cent survey of Years 7 and 8. Three schools use their PSE programmes to introduce students to the signing of whole-school contracts. The principle behind this idea is to raise awareness, and make sure everyone has a sense of their collective responsibility. All students in one school are required to sign the following contract, the words of which were decided by students in a voting procedure. In some cases all members of the school community are expected to sign a contract as exemplified by the one for Parklands High School (see p. 66).

---

**Greendale High School**

A PUPIL CONTRACT

Representing the general will of all pupils at Greendale High School after full consultation.
A. I will treat all my fellow pupils with respect.
B. I will not humiliate or hurt any other pupil physically or verbally.
C. I will do the best I can to help any pupil who is obviously being upset or hurt by one or more other pupils.

Pupil's signature _____

PARENTS:
I have read the above and will do my utmost to ensure that my son/daughter will abide by this contract.

Parent's signature _____

---

**Parklands High School**

FRIEND WATCH

A PERSONAL POLICY AGAINST BULLYING
The students, parents, staff and governors of Parklands School will
not tolerate bullying in any form.
Stopping bullying is a responsibility of everyone.
I have an important role to play in making sure bullying does not
take place.
Staff will take all reported incidents of bullying seriously and listen
to what I have told them.
Every reported incident of bullying will be recorded and dealt with
quickly.
If I witness any bullying I will do my best to stop it by getting help
and supporting the person being bullied.
I will watch out for my friends and those who seem to have few
friends.
I understand that a person who continues to bully will be expelled
from Parklands High School.
This is a policy I have helped develop and I will do my best to
make sure it works.
Signed _____
Date _____

## School culture

The signing of contracts is one example of schools using whole-school
activities as well as group and individual strategies for promoting their
anti-bullying policy. Mellor (1991) points out that for progress to be made
in the establishment of anti-bullying cultures all school personnel must
understand the anti-bullying process. Four schools specifically refer to
students having different perspectives to staff and another refers to the
problem with some 'imports who have not grown up with the ethos and
practice basic to others'. A common way of raising awareness in the whole
school is assemblies, but only one school where interviews took place use
them to 'develop informal discussion groups to open ideas'. From the
viewpoint of student respondents this may be more effective than
assemblies 'where we get shouted at and the head reprimands the whole
school after trouble'. Occasionally anti-bullying workshops are used to
open discussion with students. The National Society for the Prevention of

Cruelty to Children (NSPCC) posters and material from the DfE anti-bullying pack are popular ways of involving the whole school and four schools sent us copies of posters and leaflets of their own design.

There is evidence that such work is integral to other whole school policies. One headteacher confirmed that: 'Bullying is not seen by us as separate from pastoral and whole school policy.' Another school states at the beginning of its anti-bullying policy: 'This policy reflects the school's commitment to equal opportunities.' Thompson *et al.* (1994a) stress the importance of equal opportunities policies and reduction of racism which should involve all staff, governors and support agencies. A few schools either consciously or by default do not have an anti-bullying policy as such although they already have other behaviour policies and are using many of the above strategies. One such school has chosen not to have a written anti-bullying policy for the whole school as it already has strategies for dealing with bullying through its discipline code, its pastoral system and 'PSE' programme but gives guidelines to its staff on what constitutes bullying, and how to recognize, prevent and deal with it. Yet there is still a relatively high incidence of bullying in this school and student comments suggest that having a caring ethos is not always enough. The school's headteacher believes there is little bullying and therefore involvement in students in anti-bullying agreements, statements, peer counselling and mentoring are not necessary. He stresses instead the importance of assemblies and form tutors who establish the principles. Yet the interview data suggest that many students think that the school does not do anything to assist victims of bullying. Not many of those interviewed had confidence in their form tutors and most said assemblies had little impact on them: 'Bullying was mentioned in assembly and PSE but I can't remember it. I don't think it helped really.' Half of the 18 students interviewed had experienced bullying in some way and felt that the school had not helped. One student said: 'It was during lessons as well as break and after school.' A sixth-form head of year in another school points to the problem of 'the pupils do not really understand the wider definitions because the introductory sessions in PSE are not followed up in any depth'. In schools like these where there is a strong commitment to anti-bullying but it is not written down or shared explicitly with students, there are various interpretations and as one teacher put it, 'year heads and teams have developed their own philosophy, approach and systems'.

Westwards High School decided against calling the following an anti-bullying policy yet specifically alludes to bullying behaviour in its policy. Although this school, according to one of the tutors, has an 'improved atmosphere with pupils and staff more open and staff more prepared to share problems with other staff' interview data from a range of personnel suggest there are a number of problems still to be dealt with. Comments point to a need for INSET to provide: for 'more staff awareness on what constitutes bullying'; that 'it is difficult for teachers to empathize with bullies and their needs'; that 'a handful of teachers bully the children causing attendance problems'; and 'some female teachers are bullied by other teachers'. Peer counselling was 'tried but pupils did not opt in on this and seem to prefer talking to house tutors and coordinators'.

---

**Westwards High School**

We want our school to be a place where everyone can feel secure.

To ensure that EVERYONE has a fair deal:

- NO ONE should have to suffer name calling;
- NO ONE should have to suffer physical violence;
- NO ONE should feel victimized in any way;
- NO ONE should have to suffer racist or sexist abuse;

Remember it is the responsibility of you as STUDENTS as well as the staff to ensure harassment is not tolerated.

TELL SOMEONE

---

Questionnaire evidence suggests that a school with a caring culture may be able to support students without a specific anti-bullying policy, but an anti-bullying policy is less likely to be successful within a school which has not got consistent shared values. Those schools with policies which have clear aims, interpreted in language understood by students, publicized as tenets of good community life by all staff, and implemented through consistent practice, are more likely to be successful in achieving their aims. A head of year underlines this idea in her response that 'if there is no school policy the issue is individualized so policy issues are not faced'.

## Pastoral context

For most schools, translating their policies and guidelines into action takes place mostly within the pastoral context. This is done in a number of ways in whole school, group and individual practice including: counselling; buddy and peer counselling systems; student diaries; whole-school contracts; rewards and sanctions; and clarifying and publicizing procedures and policy. Staff in all schools acknowledge that fulfilling the aims of their policies cannot be as effective as they would wish, and point to areas where processes could work better. Practical difficulties include: a 'lack of the right environment'; 'the problems arising from lack of resources to address pupil needs'; and 'getting evidence in a way in which we can act – depending so often on what others have said'. Teachers refer to 'insufficient time to really investigate the incident or respond to the needs of the individuals concerned', for example following up by staff in one school on their students' diaries. Another teacher comments: 'We frequently have to deal with problems where we cannot really track down and sort out the relationships and what really happened – the truth eludes us.' Where peer counselling is established to provide additional help sometimes there is 'a loss of heart if it is not used by the tutors and children'. Many bullies and victims are unwilling to disclose their real feelings, to share their difficulties and recognize their own problems and there is much evidence that some of these students are actually ignored by the normative group.

Compton and Baizerman (1991), stress the role of counselling in overcoming problems of at-risk children. Only one school in the partnership has a designated school counsellor, though teachers in several schools have been on counselling courses. One tutor felt strongly the need for 'anger counselling'. A few schools refer to specific counselling procedures as well as the ongoing support from tutors and pastoral staff. One school pays for a consultancy group to lead a 'Conflict Club' and at least two schools have a 'Drop In' service run by their school nurses. Ten schools have set up peer counselling services with varying success. At one end of the spectrum is a project established over six years where peer counsellors reported to their tutor that their work 'can remedy and resolve their own conflicts' as well as helping others, and at the other end where a peer counselling system was considered 'not successful because pupils relate better to staff'.

Roland (1993) discusses bullying management in terms of splitting and reuniting bullies and then following with cooperative behaviour patterns. This is a systematic approach based on a teacher as mediator between, parents, class and the anti-bullying structure. Sexual harassment is an issue which according to Stein (1995) needs to be included in the curriculum and which needs adult intervention. The school with the counsellor sent us an account of this type of intervention whereby she counselled separately the group of boys who were doing the harassing and the girls who were the recipients. She brought the two groups together in a highly structured format so that each side could tell the other specifically what they did and did not like about its behaviour. In addition they could, without interruption, state what future behaviour they wanted from the other group. At the end of the session both groups appreciated being given the chance to give their sides of the story fully and be listened to. They felt the counsellor had not taken sides and had been fair to both groups. In their separate groups they were helped to release their feelings and think more clearly about the opposite sex and what they wanted in relation to them. They left the session together, talking in a friendly way and a few days later the counsellor gave them both sets of written agreements. Subsequently there was no more sexual harassment and no awkwardness during tutor time or lessons. The counsellor sums up her account as follows:

> What pleased me most was: the harassment stopped as a result of the young women deciding that it had to do so and they took the necessary steps to see to it; and that it ceased not as the result of a threat or an order but because both parties concerned had an understanding of what had been happening and saw for themselves why it must not happen again.

## Getting practice known

Clarifying and publicizing procedures and policy so that they reach teachers, governors, dinner supervisors and parents as well as the students themselves is a high priority in those schools which intend to have maximum impact, though several schools do not give this priority for fear of adverse publicity. Many schools produce handouts for students and we were sent four of these as well as six posters reminding all students of the basic ethos of 'care and consideration for others', that 'bullying is not necessarily physical' and that 'pupils are to be treated fairly by all, all treated equally, and all should be free to disclose incidents to staff'. Some schools give clear guidance to every group of people in their school communities, such as one school which has detailed guidelines for visitors, pupils, support staff, site supervisors and janitors, lunch-time supervisors, teaching staff and parents. Another has guidance for staff written by students which is published in the staff handbook. Smith and Sharp (1994) in their study of the Sheffield project comment on the importance of keeping the issues alive. Pupil interviews suggest strongly that they need to be reminded regularly of set procedures, opportunities for counselling and other aspects of policy on bullying. In many cases these are posted around the school and made known through student and teacher news-sheets. Four schools mention that letters are sent home, at least two include the policy in the prospectus and two specifically refer to photographs of peer helpers around the school.

## Monitoring and evaluation

The extent of changes in values or relationships cannot be objectively measured. However, it is possible to find out the nature, frequency and location of bullying incidences and it is essential to do so in order to be able to counter bullying successfully in school. This can be done by conducting regular surveys and by keeping bullying incident records filled in by teachers and students. A few schools have embarked upon this process but it is still in its infancy in most cases. The school staff who were interviewed were asked to outline the process of monitoring the new policies within their schools and of the 81 responses only 14 recognized that incidents of bullying were logged and only four said that they were used to assess the policy. Most commonly the pastoral staff of schools include 'a regular agenda item on bullying where we swap information and try to achieve consistency in the way we act' or 'a termly review of all pupils with the form tutor and year head so that we spot problems and act before the crisis stage'.

Ahmad *et al*. (1991) used questionnaires adapted from Olweus's self-reporting inventories both before and after intervention strategies in 24 schools in Sheffield and the results showed many positive effects. Professionally developed surveys have been used in four Keele Partnership schools as a means of finding out the situation, planning action and following up to find out the effectiveness of strategies. Four others have developed their own questionnaires to use in sections of the school from time to time to see 'how we have managed to change attitudes over the last couple of years' and 'to give us some indicator of the way in which pupils see things'.

Bullying Incident Records are another way of monitoring the level of bullying behaviour. Making a written report of the incident on a proforma is both reassuring to the person who has reported the incident and helps clarify what happened, yet only four of the responding schools specifically mention the use of them. The main issues to be considered regarding the use of such forms concern collation to ensure cross-referencing, the retention of information on student files and the use of information in the monitoring and evaluation process to find out what patterns are emerging.

Monitoring seems to be a random process in most schools with many relying on subjective reports from pastoral staff. Most of the respondents speak in terms of 'the increase in confidence', 'the readiness of pupils to come and tell staff of their problems', 'the frequency with which pupils will approach staff is an indicator of trust', and that 'whilst there are no statistics as yet there have been fewer phone calls from parents since the first term, and we have watched the attendance pattern'. One school's headteacher believes its five-year rotation of year heads should give more opportunities for monitoring students' relationships in this way. Perhaps the most important monitoring is that 'of watching the progress of bully and victim', and of 'trying to see the relationship between the wider use of anti-bullying and results in more effective teaching'. As far as student respondents are concerned, anything which makes the learning environment safer is considered worth while.

The impact of change can only be evaluated through evidence of a changed environment for students. The responses from staff in the surveyed schools suggest that there has been considerable improvement with a reduction in the number of reported cases of serious bullying and the long-term impact this has had on students. Most schools report less than ten serious incidents during the past year although they also provide evidence that not all cases are serious, especially where 'the isolated events are effectively dealt with' and that problems may therefore be more widespread but 'with a high nuisance value'. It is worth noting that there seems to be a popular assumption that the number of disclosures indicates the actual number of bullying incidences, yet our survey reveals the contrary. Several schools where staff believe they have a low incidence have a relatively high number compared to the norm for other schools in the partnership investigation.

As well as reporting 'a decline from the overtly physical' and 'fewer reported cases, and usually less severe than in previous years', schools also continue to report problems for 'the lowest 20 per cent of the ability range', 'the younger children who seem to experience more bullying' and 'the poor or less able despite all that we do to maintain policy'. There is also a continuing concern regarding: 'too much corridor abuse'; 'problems taking place out of school such as on buses where seating is a problem'; 'girls suffering from body criticism'; 'non-uniform days where there are problems of poor turnout'; 'the growth of more subtle and psychologically damaging bullying amongst the able pupils'; 'neighbourhoods where there are different values and dysfunctional families resulting in teachers having a greater tolerance threshold'; 'a no grassing ethos amongst pupils and where problems are sorted out by families'; and the difficulties of 'sharing information about pupils while protecting confidentiality'. In short the problems may be changing in their nature and seriousness. This exemplifies the need for frequent re-evaluation of the content and impact of published policies. In Fullan's terms (1991), the stage of institutionalization may allow a policy to become part of the fabric of the organization. If it is all so well embedded that the detail does not require updating, all well and good, but there are few schools so stable that they would not benefit from some review of all policies over a cycle of years.

---

**Reflection**  Schools are complex organizations. Fullan (1991) suggests that change may begin in pilot areas and then eventually become part of the embedded culture of the school. What inhibiting factors are likely to prevent or delay this in a school or group known to you?

# REACHING THE PARENTS

## Partnerships

In considering the development of policies within schools there has been
varying reference to the part played by parents. They may contribute to
policy development through membership of parents' committees, or in
one school, through being given the opportunity to respond to a proposed
draft policy document. In two of the thirteen schools studied in detail,
parents had attended meetings with the staff before proposals were final-
ized. Much depends upon the reciprocity of relationship between the staff
of the school and the parents. Stone (1995) outlines the difficulties overcome in establishing understanding in an area of socio-economic deprivation with many pupils from ethnic minority homes. These include the
problems of communication, the tensions between majority and minority
culture and the lack of social self-confidence in parents.

There are additional difficulties in this involvement in establishing anti-
bullying policies. Schools have difficulty in persuading parents that 'do
not understand wider definitions', that some non-physical action may be
hurtful although they are likely to understand physical bullying. 'Funny
looks' and 'name-calling have a considerable personal impact but they are
difficult to detect' and action against such behaviour is seen by some parents to be unduly harsh. At the other extreme, some parental expectation
of good social interaction 'exceeds the bounds of reasonableness in expecting behaviour which is not part of the normal metaphorical rough and
tumble of the playground'. One form teacher comments that 'care is
needed in the use of language because highlighting the problem may lead
the public to think that there is a problem when none exists'. This then
leads to differing expectations – of victims that there will be action to meet
their complaints, and of bullies that their actions have not been other than
'joking or messing about'. This is worsened where there is a conflict
between the school view 'of a secure environment and the problems of
the neighbourhood way of doing things' especially where 'they have a

non-cooperative stance towards the school' or where the social mores of the neighbourhood see bullying as a 'natural phenomenon and not something which they can influence'. The involvement of external agencies such as social services or the police in solving difficulties is, in the words of one head, 'inherently difficult because they are changing to a more hands-off approach at a time when we are being urged to be more active in settling issues between pupils and their families'. This has been investigated in relationship to pupil achievement (Ziegler 1987) and the link between expectation and social class whilst significant is not the only determinant of mutual understanding. Where child–parent, and parent–school interaction is based upon common understanding by parents and teachers of the aims of the school policy, implementation is likely to be more effective.

Problems also arise from pupil and parent views of necessary intervention to secure a resolution of difficulties. Many parents of victims expect immediate and severe sanctions but 'they will not discuss the problems with year heads or tutors who know the children involved much better – they see the head as the only serious contact'. In the eyes of many parents, some 'teachers have too high a tolerance threshold' and they see lack of intervention as weakness when the counterargument of staff is that 'problems do often resolve themselves in a short period of time given open discussion'. For one tutor 'perceived inadequate dealing is worse than no action at all' and evidence suggests that 'many adolescent girls who have been the subject of exclusion from the group, or name-calling feel that they have been dismissed by teachers to whom they complain'. Of the 98 incidents commented upon in interviews, the 22 episodes of physical bullying appear to have been more satisfactorily dealt with than the 76 episodes of social exclusion, taunting and mishandling property. This is believed to be because teachers act 'through separating the pupils, finding out what has gone wrong, sending them to the head and then letting the parents know'.

---

**Reflection**   There appears to be a view that physical bullying is more serious than other forms of anti-social behaviour. Does this reflect the childhood experiences of teachers, or cultural norms in society? Will these change in the course of time?

---

Associated problems arise from the 'difficulty for many teachers to empathize with the bully and his or her needs – often there is not enough time to deal with both sides and the bully may need more mentoring and counselling than the victim but the view is that they should be helped first'. Where training of peer and sixth-form counsellors has been undertaken schools are able to make some additional help available but even 'this brings problems when we train the counsellors and then the need diminishes as a result of policies at work in the lower school'. Parents may not readily appreciate the involvement of peer counsellors and they may, by their influence on their children, inhibit the readiness of pupils to talk to peers. In this respect too, many bullies and their victims are unwilling to disclose their real feelings, to share their difficulties or to recognize their own problems with peers, staff or parents – and there is much evidence that some victims whilst not bullied are actually ignored by the normative group. Parents may not be ready to understand the hurt imposed by social exclusion even if they take action in defence of physical bullying. Even here there is a dilemma for 'where physical retaliation is taught in the home and expected by the parents, appreciation of more gradual changes in relationships between pupils are minimal'. In this situation, the resolution of issues through the pastoral curriculum may be hampered 'because all that they do is talk, they don't actually solve anything'. Parents appear to want evidence of decisive action against bullies – unless their child is the accused. Levine (1993) outlines the need for care in handling this tension and stresses the importance of dialogue related to the development of bully and victim rather than protracted attempts at apportioning blame.

In these circumstances partnership development is very difficult. Rutherford and Billig (1995) see social behaviour as an issue when the early and middle secondary years are a watershed in pupil development and that effective liaison with parents requires mutual understanding of authority, independence and relationships so that teachers and parents are starting from the same base. The difficulty is that not all parents are willing to be part of the partnership and many become critical of the 'official line'. The role of form tutors as link personnel, the encouragement of the involvement of all parents, the use of parents as support for and contributors to the curriculum, and effective staff development to promote good communications are all important in securing a higher level of parent participation. Garrity (1994) urges schools to develop training for staff to work with parents in establishing shared understanding rather than accepting that parents really appreciate what the school aims to achieve. This requires planning for action within the context of the social background of the school.

## The social background

In Chapter 1, we outlined the relationship between the perceived occurrence of bullying behaviour and the social background of the families in the surveys. This research also shows that whilst an average of 40.7 per cent of parents believe that the school deals very effectively with bullying, 5.6 per cent of the more affluent parents believe that improvement is urgently required whilst 11.2 per cent of those tending to financial difficulty or receiving benefits believe that this is true. Of the former group, 16 per cent believe that their child has been bullied whilst 26 per cent of the less affluent perceive that their child suffers. More seriously though, twice as many of the poorer group think that the bullying is frequent. If this is so there are questions to be asked about the communication between teachers and social groups. The practice in three of the thirteen schools in which staff were interviewed shows that there is some compensatory counselling for families which recognizes that it is likely that parents as well as pupils have difficulty in explaining their problems. Wilczenski (1994) urges that this counselling should be undertaken as part of community provision for family therapy. In only one of the sample schools is there provision for a counsellor to undertake any outreach work. Lowenstein (1978a,b) outlined the relationship between an adverse home environment, characterized by a high level of verbal and physical abuse, and subsequent bullying behaviour and, in working with two Caribbean communities, Ramoutar (1995) substantiates the view that socio-economic status is a determinant of bullying potential. Evans (1994) stresses the importance of assisting pupils from such backgrounds to develop self-esteem within school as a compensatory measure.

Pupils are aware that differences in financial and social conditions may affect the perceptions that others in the school have of them. One comments that 'pupils pick on those who don't wear clothes as good as the rest', another that 'you are expected to dress in clothes that are in fashion all the time and we haven't got enough money to do so . . . everyone's got Kickers and we'll never be able to afford any'. In the questionnaire responses pupils say that parents almost always support an average of 44 per cent of the cohort although this declines from 55 per cent in Year 7 to 38 per cent in Year 11, and with equality for boys and girls. Schools have shown that they recognize the implication of social differences through 'the use of uniform which can be purchased at any of a range of suppliers' and 'careful planning of non-uniform events to overcome the problems of the have and have-nots'.

## Parental attitudes

As pupils get older, they tend to tell their parents less about their life at school and effective liaison depends upon the subjective views of pupils and the communication of these to parents. The interview evidence also makes it clear that many pupils are facing a double battle in establishing a secure basis for living in school because they feel unsupported within their homes. This may be because pupils fail to match up to parental expectations in some form, or because they feel misunderstood. It is possible, perhaps, that those pupils who have a lower self-image may also experience some distancing from their parents. About 24 per cent of both boys and girls believe that their parents are strict or very strict, and slightly less think that too much is expected of them and that they are pushed too hard. These might contribute to a feeling of inadequacy such that 14 per cent would like to leave home, 17 per cent easily get upset at home and 14 per cent feel that they are a disappointment to their parents. The possible indicators of stability show that many more respondents feel that they have a good home life with about 70 per cent believing that parents do consider their feelings, that they are understood by their parents, that they enjoy parental support in school and that they feel happy at home. Table 6.1 summarizes these responses.

Parental reaction to bullying events follows the levels of support suggested in child–parent relationships. Twenty per cent of respondents are encouraged to fight back in the event of trouble – not necessarily by the same parents as those who might undermine self-confidence; 44 per cent believe that their parents would talk to someone about life at school and 30 per cent say that their parents have actually complained. The culture against which this takes place does, however, affect attitudes with 46 per cent of parents prepared to smack their children, and there is less than total support for their children with over 30 per cent only conditionally prepared to believe their offspring. Young people with low self-esteem and poor parental support appear from the interviews to be more likely to 'have to sort things out for myself' or 'go along with the gang because I am frightened to break away from them'. The experience of Emma in Year 9 illustrates this.

> I was very unhappy because the girls ganged up on me and called me names when I moved about the school but I knew that my mum would say to sort it out and give them one back . . . but I couldn't do it, and I had been warned to stay out of trouble and so it was better to just stay miserable. I had been suicidal and I will get that way again because there is nobody to believe me.

**Table 6.1** Student perception of relationship to parents ($n = 4596$)

| Characteristic | Mostly (%) | Sometimes (%) | Rarely (%) |
|---|---|---|---|
| Parents consider my feelings | 72 | 21 | 7 |
| Parents expect too much of me | 21 | 33 | 46 |
| Parents understand me | 62 | 26 | 11 |
| Parents are pushing me | 17 | 29 | 54 |
| Parents support me in schools | 73 | 19 | 7 |
| I seem to disappoint parents | 14 | 25 | 61 |
| I get easily upset at home | 17 | 27 | 57 |
| I would like to leave home | 14 | 22 | 64 |
| Siblings get a better deal | 23 | 31 | 46 |

Open comment and interview data reveals much of the impact of developing self-esteem in managing adverse situations. One of the Year 9 girls commented:

> I get bullied at school and have been so for the past three years. Its started to wear off now but they always find something nasty to say about me or push me. They know I can't fight back, I haven't got the strength to. I would like it to stop but it's impossible. I can't talk to my mum and dad, they don't listen and they are fed up with hearing me moan all the time. I also hate seeing other people get bullied and I'd like to stop them. I am only 13 and the youngest girl in my year. I can't talk to anyone . . . the teachers just tell me to ignore them but I can't.

And from an older boy:

> some lads in my year were name-calling, they do it all the time and they think that it's funny. It hurts people's feelings and it put me down so much that sometimes I don't want to go into lessons but other friends tell me to ignore it and they may get fed up – it still makes me feel different.

The interview data show that pupil–parent action follows a spectrum of belief in their children varying from 'if I tell my mum and dad they will come down to the school with all guns blazing but that usually causes more trouble than enough' through to the complaint that 'if I tell them they think that I may be to blame and they won't do anything about it'. Much depends on the nature of parent and child relationships. Evidence from the interviews shows that older pupils believe that 'unless we are in the wrong we should be asked whether we want our parents involved or not because there are times when I would prefer to make a stand on my own . . . it just isn't easy to talk to my mum and dad at the moment'. The need for care is explained by one girl who 'has a problem because I come from a single-parent family and unless I really had to I wouldn't want to involve my mum in more worry especially if we would only be told to keep away from the girls who cause me difficulty – I know that already'. Four interviewees, all from urban estates, spoke of long-running interfamily problems which would be worsened as a result of parental involvement and saw history repeated in situations where 'there had been trouble when my mum and dad were at the school when it was a sec. mod. [secondary modern] and they have never got on with the family – they have always fought in one way or another'. A further four spoke of the ineffective consequences of action summed up as 'not making any difference because the kids and their parents go on as they have done for years'. In the event, time appears to have been a healer in about half the narratives and the hopelessness of the negative effect of finally being left to survive is summed up in one comment that 'I knew that my mum would go to the school and that she said that she would help but then told me that the only way to settle the matter was to give them one!' Overall there is greater confidence in parental ability to support pupils in settling matters in the questionnaire responses with 73 per cent believing that they would 'always or mostly' have parental support but even so 7 per cent believe that this would 'rarely or never occur' – a significant minority. The extended family ties are shown in the fact that 27 of the 115 interviewed said that they would want older brothers (10) or sisters (17) involved, mostly as an advocate or physical support but one boy and one girl saw them as listeners. Two further respondents saw that sibling involvement could lead to further aggravation but the narratives supplied by three girls in one school suggest that the out-of-school culture is more violent than that in school and that many pupils are waiting to graduate into the life of the estate and the town.

## Taking action

Schools have taken action to ensure that parental confidence is maintained in three ways. Initially the problems are identified within the school situation and all the schools in the cohort indicate that they expect to work with parents at some stage in dealing with serious or repeated bullying behaviour. Guidance to teachers to ensure that there is consistency in the way in which they work with parents is given by one school which always meets with parents following any complaint. The evidence from all the schools where policy was discussed suggests that pupils are quick to see any variation in the way in which incidents are dealt with and the structure is offered as a means of promoting fairness.

---

**Forest Bank School**

**Dealing with parents of bullies – guidance for teaching staff**

(a) Seek support for school action in involving parents.
(b) Parents show disapproval of behaviour (if they also punish, be careful they do not go too far) – discuss joint approach.
(c) Why bully? Delicate issue and needs careful handling:
 • older brother or sister who bullies?
 • violent parents?
 • bully a witness to abuse at home?
 • parents punish inconsistently?
 • bully has been or still is a victim of other bullies?
(d) Point out implications for future:
 • likely low achievement at school

- criminal acts
- affect on career
- aggressive children grow up to become violent partners and citizens

(e)  Any signs of aggressiveness, emotional outbursts at home? Identify causes. Parents overbearing or not dominant enough etc.?

(f)  Help parents devise strategies to change child's behaviour.

(g)  Parents helped to understand reward of non-violent behaviour.

(h)  If problem addressed in the home, then greater likelihood of success in school.

A second approach is to advise parents that bullying may occur and to offer materials based upon research findings. Parents who realize or suspect that their child is being bullied at school will probably experience many painful emotions themselves and feel powerless to act and comments from interviews indicate that intervention is often only at the point of crisis. Pervin (1995) has shown that it is important not to project this sense of powerlessness on their child or act out their emotions in front of her/him. If the child thinks their parent will be upset, angry, bewildered or embarrassed, they are less likely to disclose what has happened to them. So that parents can respond helpfully to their child's situation they will probably need to find some support for themselves as well as for their child as outlined by Elliot (1986) and latterly by Maynard (1993) who has considered the serious problems in the USA. Several of the sample schools issue advice to parents at the time of pupil entry to the school in an attempt to pre-empt problems.

**Cathedral High School**

**Extract from letter to parents regarding bullying**

A few general guidelines gathered from texts on the subject are as follows:

- be aware of signs and symptoms of bullying – unwillingness to attend school; a pattern of headaches/stomach aches; equipment gone missing; requests for extra pocket money; damaged clothes or bruising;
- ask your child directly if you suspect they are being bullied;
- listen to and believe your child;

- find out the facts when told about a bullying incident;
- keep a written record of bullying including who, what, when and where;
- do not overreact – instead be calm and optimistic about supporting your child pointing out there is nothing wrong with her/him and that it happens to many people;
- give your child the chance to vent her/his feelings about being bullied;
- encourage your child to invite others home to help her/him make friends;
- take an interest in your child's social life at school;
- inform school of any recent upsets which may be contributing to unusual behaviour or distress in your child;
- be involved with school policy and work in partnership with the school;
- talk to teachers and find out if there is one responsible for discipline and anti-bullying;
- if you think your child is being bullied inform the school immediately and arrange an interview with the member of staff responsible;
- devise strategies with staff that will help your child and provide her/him with support at home and school;
- encourage children to talk to teachers;
- do not encourage your child to fight back as this goes against her/his nature and makes matters worse – instead encourage her/him to recruit friends;
- if your child is aggressive encourage her/him to find other ways of behaving;
- help your child practise strategies such as: saying or shouting 'no!'; or walking or running away with confidence;
- do not agree to keep the bullying a secret;
- if you are not helped by staff, tell a parent governor about your problem;
- if you receive no help from the governors inform the LEA;
- if the problem occurs outside school arrange for a solicitor's letter to be sent to the bully's parents, informing them of the legal consequences of the recurrence of the bullying.

A third approach is to use school–home communications such as newsletters associated with occasional open meetings as a means of alerting parents to policy development and to current issues within the school. Such approaches, are, however, dependent upon the willingness of parents to use opportunities which are offered and for many 'crossing the threshold except to get specific detail of a child's progress requires a greater degree of confidence in their ability to be part of the school community than occurs in reality – they still see the teachers in the light of their own experience as pupils'. Pipho (1994) suggests that this is the most important single issue to be resolved in establishing effective partnership in policymaking and implementation.

---

**Reflection**   What is 'the reality of the school community'? Can the reality be changed either as a result of external agencies or internal policy development?

---

## Parental intervention

Whilst parents may understand school policy and the procedures which are followed as part of anti-bullying education there is evidence that their involvement in problem-solving is not welcomed by many pupils and this has an undermining effect on the success of policy development in any partnership. In the event of threats or physical hurt, 30 per cent of the respondents in the survey would tell their father and 44 per cent their mother, but there is a marked decline in the extent of telling which is half as prevalent in Year 11 as it is in Year 7, and in gender with 32 per cent of boys prepared to talk to their father compared with 27 per cent of the girls, and 37 per cent of the boys ready to talk to their mother compared with 51 per cent of the girls.

The comparatively low percentage of pupils prepared to talk to parents is reflected in interview comments. One boy believes that 'much depends on the way in which families can sort things out . . . some parents have an interest and will help to clear up their problems but others leave you to get on alone'. Another says 'parents have a right to know but they may not always do anything' and 'they know you better than the teachers'. Reluctance to involve parents appears to be related to one or more of three adolescent views. Independence is shown in the statement that 'the involvement of parents is not a good thing because it is my life and I am ready to sort things out for myself'. Potential embarrassment is a recurrent view of girls who fear 'that having my mum involved may not be a real help because she does not understand the way things work in school'. The most commonly cited reason for not involving parents is that 'they do not help the situation . . . the bully knows that you will bring them in and then you are called names like grass'. However, if parental involvement is initiated by the school it seems to be more acceptable to adolescent society – a consequence of action rather than a reason for it.

**Reflection** Parental involvement generally declines with pupil maturation. What limitations does this impose on potential home–school partnerships?

Consideration of the data shows that parental involvement is more readily accepted by both pupils and staff in some schools than in others. If an index of favourable comment about parent involvement is used for the responding schools, one school achieves 0.3, three 0.4, one 0.5, four 0.6, three 0.8 and one 0.9. Evidence from the lowest-scoring school reflects a lack of consistent practice and the involvement of parents as a last resort with a certain disillusionment on the part of pupils in terms of 'not much help if they only tell you to keep away from the bully' and 'I wouldn't tell my parents because they think that I am unable to cope and if they went to school it would be worse for me'. The higher-scoring schools have policies which involve consideration of the role of parents as part of the personal and social education programme and in one school tutorial work has reinforced the partnership view. The effectiveness of the partnership is shown in the comment of a pupil from one of these schools who says:

> I think that if bullies are caught they should be made to see what sort of a person they are, because I used to bully in Years 8 and 9 because I was being bullied . . . my dad sat me down and told me which sort of person I was becoming and it made me realize this and I stopped . . . I have not threatened or bullied anyone since.

The pupils who were interviewed were asked to consider the effectiveness of the involvement of parents in settling in-school disputes. Of the 115 interviewed, 31 boys and 21 girls had had parents involved. Of these, eight males and five females consider that they were asked if they wished parents to be involved, and four males and three females believe that intervention was a final resort following a period of ineffective help from teachers. Intervention was perceived to have been effective by 20 per cent of the males interviewed, and 42 per cent of the females, and to have led to better parent and teacher contact by 3 per cent of the males and 35 per cent of the females. Twenty per cent of the males considered that involvement led to an increase in interfamily problems particularly where relationships with older or younger siblings had been poor. This was less evident with the females who were interviewed. One deputy head summed up difficulties in securing a more consistent parental involvement as 'many parents have a non-cooperative stance regarding the school and attempt to settle things in their own way after we have sorted out the problem within school'. Once again, we return to the problem of establishing a level of understanding by parents of the culture of the school and to reconcile this with the culture of the community.

# 7 THE COMMUNITY

## One community or many?

Our conversations with the young people in the sample schools underlined the importance of the community context as a factor which determines corporate attitudes to anti-social behaviour. The Keele questionnaire survey did not directly ask about the life of young people outside school but the open comments and the interview data gave valuable evidence to support the view that, although the school may work to eradicate bullying, there are features of the external culture which inhibit attitudinal change. These include the parental view of survival, the peer pressure exerted by gangs out of school when older members dominate, and the efficacy of police, social service and other agencies, and the youth service in supporting positive community perspectives. In all these aspects, it seems that where the school tends to serve a close community it is more able to affect culture beyond the school gates. This may be true even though it may be working against adverse circumstances and contrasts with the expressed hope of some schools that 'whilst we want to do something to help all our youngsters to play a full part in the life of their community we are not able to do so because each village, each area, and each knot of families has their own set of community values and the further you are from the school the more difficult it is to influence what happens'.

Several of the case study schools have a high level of community integration with the building acting as a social and cultural centre for the neighbourhood, and providing a base for adult evening classes, daytime leisure and access to further education courses where space permits, and evening youth work. This helps blur the distinction between parents and the community at large but in more dispersed areas, and in schools which draw upon a wider catchment than the immediate neighbourhood of the school the 'stakeholders', whether governors, parents or the community at large, are geographically spread and may be culturally diverse. Karpicke and Murphy (1996) see this as a situation requiring greater efforts on the part of a school to transmit and develop its shared values to the community it serves. Kelly and Cohn (1988) in considering the life of ethnic minorities identify the existence of community groups within the larger area and point to the much greater incidence of anti-social behaviour towards the Asian groups. The recognition of this by pupils is shown in the comment that 'I do not suffer bullying except that they call me names because I am an Asian but some racism is to be expected' and in the view that 'there will always be fighting between English and Asian groups out of school'. The comments imply that there is some level of expected, and even accepted, racial intolerance within the minority community. However, the staff of schools recognize this grouping and undertake compensatory measures, for example: through the use of teachers who are aware of the culture of ethnic groups as liaison staff; agreeing to membership of community and neighbourhood development committees; providing minority language communications to parents; and establishing integrative courses which focus on pupil development.

---

**Reflection**   Why do minority groups become excluded from community relationships? Can schools do anything to build cultural bridges? If so, is this more difficult in rural areas?

---

Intervention denies the existence of a deeper problem in the 'anti-school view of some of our parents who have come from families with a deep suspicion of school as a group of people interfering with their way of doing things'. This is shown in the view of one year tutor that 'we have been hampered in developing an anti-bullying policy because of a fundamental view that "grassing" is wrong and that matters like bullying are best left to the families to sort out'. An education welfare officer comments on the 'family feuds which have been going on for two or three generations and which are sustained out of school'. A deputy head commented on the 'uncooperative stance taken by many parents towards the school in dealing with bullying which they believe should be left to them to settle with the other families involved but if we don't act then we are in the wrong'.

Any school which is attempting to establish policies involving the community may be taking on the problems of that community as well as those of the school itself and, where the cultural values of the home conflict with those of the school, progress is inhibited. Part of the difficulty lies in the failure of the community to recognize that there is a two-way relationship and that whilst employers, residents and civic groups expect that the school will instil the highest standards in the young people there are clear indications that out-of-school youth, recreational and sporting activities which would help development are often denied for funding reasons.

Randall (1996) details the potential of community links but these require the willingness of both school and community to participate. The three schools which have accepted that they have problems in working with their communities have less reported incidents of bullying in the survey than in other schools, whilst two of three schools with highly developed anti-bullying policies have high levels of reporting in the survey as shown in Table 7.1. This may indicate that 'tough homes breed tough kids' and that the readiness to report incidents is greater where awareness has been raised. This may be enhanced where anonymity in surveys allows for greater freedom to respond. It may also be related to the fact that the disadvantaged tend to have a high tolerance level and appear to be much more reticent in approaching the school as a means of settling interfamily problems. There is extensive research (Downey and Coyne 1990; Byrne 1994b) to indicate that home life may not only lead to bullying behaviour but may also promote the view that victimization is part of the pattern of life. 'You have to learn to stand up for yourself because nobody will do it for you' was the comment from one pupil from a disadvantaged background. As with our comments on racism, there is a danger that some of the so-called immutable facts of community life are accepted as normal – our evidence is that pupils suffer in the long run as a result.

One of the most important influences on social behaviour in school is the relationship between pupils and dinner supervisors, cleaners and other ancillary staff. Almost invariably these are members of the community drawn from the neighbourhood and with an understanding of the views of the community and the school. Their importance as a source of information and as an influence in the local network is recognized by several schools who operate training schemes for these staff and who have established procedures by which they are able to inform and influence pastoral staff. They are key people in the lives of school pupils at school. They are often in places where bullying occurs and they have a crucial role

**Table 7.1** Percentage of respondents reporting being bullied 'often' in six sample schools according to community characteristics

| Community | Physical bullying (%) | Verbal teasing (%) | Property damage (%) |
|---|---|---|---|
| Adverse rural | 4.0 | 23.6 | 8.5 |
| Adverse urban | 3.8 | 26.0 | 10.3 |
| Adverse mixed | 3.3 | 18.8 | 5.3 |
| Supportive mixed | 3.0 | 19.5 | 7.3 |
| Supportive rural | 10.3 | 27.8 | 9.6 |
| Supportive urban | 11.7 | 26.2 | 7.6 |
| Mean of all 25 schools | 6.0 | 25.0 | 7.1 |

in dealing with it. Despite their vital importance in the life of the school, in most cases they have a low status compared to teaching staff. Lunch-time supervisors in particular have very difficult supervisory roles and this is not helped if they have a low status in pupils' eyes. It is therefore important that the role of these key workers are seen by all as equally valuable as the role of teaching staff and that they contribute to school policy and are kept fully informed on all anti-bullying work. By consulting and involving lunch-time supervisors and other non-teaching staff they realize that their views and insights are very important, there is an increase in self-esteem and this results in a greater commitment to and success in their work. Problems may arise when the open nature of discussion leads to possible breaks of confidentiality or when the ancillary workers attempt to enforce their own form of discipline. One pupil commented that 'sometimes the dinner ladies can be bullies themselves' and a deputy head suggested that much more care is needed in the recruitment of untrained staff who may not understand the ethos of the school and in establishing basic values in subsequent training which is offered to them. Downlands School gives guidelines to lunch-time supervisors. The view of the school in this situation is that ancillary staff as community members may be more effective 'in speaking the same language' than intervening teachers who may not be associated with the area and who may not know the local culture.

---

**Downlands School**

GUIDELINES ON THE IMPLEMENTATION OF OUR ANTI-BULLYING POLICY: LUNCHTIME SUPERVISORS

BULLYING IS THE WILFUL, CONSCIOUS DESIRE TO HURT OR THREATEN OR FRIGHTEN SOMEONE ELSE

WHAT IF . . .

1  I see or receive a report of damage to property, graffiti, vandalism or borrowing without permission?
2  I see or receive a report of silent pressure, shunning/ignoring, group pressure or invasion of privacy?
3  I hear or receive a report of name calling, ridicule, rumour/malicious gossip, notepassing or heckling?
4  I see or receive a report of fighting, extortion, intimidation, physical violence or incitement?

I MUST REPORT IT TO A SENIOR MEMBER OF THE TEACHING STAFF WHO WILL COMPLETE A BULLYING INCIDENT SHEET. IF I FEEL ABLE, I CAN EXPLAIN THE INCIDENT'S OFFENSIVE NATURE TO THE INDIVIDUAL

In understanding the community culture, Batsche and Knoff (1994) refer to the family factors which may prompt bullying behaviour summed up in the need to survive in an adverse atmosphere. This is spelt out by Schwartz (1993) in terms of exposure of children to harsh punishment, violence between family members, aggressive role models, marital conflict and family exposure to stressful events such as loss of job, loss of home, illness or death. Our interview evidence suggests that despite these problems the tie to the home is very strong and the pupil expects to be supported by parents or siblings if any difficulties occur. Of the 115 interviewees, 27 would be supported by older brothers and sisters, and 43 by parents. In this situation family ties may be such that school intervention cannot be successful because the reality of a situation is subjectively interpreted by both school and family and defensive stances may then inhibit reason. One head felt that the school was expecting families in the community to adopt standards which were at variance with their protective culture, despite the evidence of adverse home circumstances. Gleeson (1994) explores this as a possible explanation for truancy and it may be that families accept the reality of bullying because they feel that they are victims of a society which bullies them through poor employment opportunities and consequent poverty. Disadvantaged pupils fighting for survival at home and out of school may find that they do not fit the society at school. This was illustrated by one interviewee who spoke of the pressures within and outside school on one girl who 'had poor clothes and they were all having a go at her so much that she took an overdose of asthma inhalant at home, she had had enough . . . she doesn't come to the school any more'. As the bully delimits the areas of the playground which less strong pupils may inhabit, it is possible that a culture clash may alienate some pupils to the extent that they are denied their educational opportunities.

At the same time, there may be tension between those with comparatively affluent homes and the general run of the school neighbourhood. This is illustrated in two of the schools which are situated as the only secondary school in market towns and which both draw on children from scattered rural communities, affluent new housing developments and council estates. Interview evidence suggests that social groups within school mirror the associations outside school – similarity of interests, for example horse-riding, may promote a group who in the words of other pupils 'have the lot', whilst the 'in-town girls get together and go to the disco every weekend when we can't get there'. The work of the school in promoting the anti-bullying message may be hampered by the existence of differing communities. Schools, in approaching this problem may decide to offer little beyond the school gates although they may be ready to welcome the community to use their resources. This view is reflected in the encouragement given to parents to approach the police regarding any incident which occurs beyond the school day in three of the schools. The school may however, join with other educational groups to foster a community awareness and to develop allies in that community, or it may become allied to other agencies on a broad front in the hope of securing a fundamental change in attitudes.

## The school as the community centre

Stone (1995) outlines the way in which a school serving a depressed area of San Diego, California, has been turned round through its community involvement. The problems of Central Elementary School are far greater than those of any of the sample schools but in an age when pupil recruitment is important the way in which anti-social behaviour was managed provides some indication of successful strategies. The guiding principles of the school as a focal point for the life of the community, of flexibility to allow for staffing to meet community needs, and for the school to see that it could only be understood if it reached out to its own community, are mirrored in the mission of two schools serving the most disadvantaged areas within the current investigation. A fundamental tactic for Central Elementary School was to harness the wishes of parents to achieve something better for their children. All three schools recognize that they serve geographically identifiable areas and have a cultural homogeneity which enables them to work more readily with the parents for whom the school is recognizable, is part of the tradition of educational service within the area, and where both youth and adult education facilities are available. This does, however, pose problems in that pupils see the school as an authoritarian institution and countercultures may develop within the neighbourhood as a result. In the words of one interviewee 'we don't want anything to do with school when we leave it because we can meet on the estate – around the bus stop for example – and we want something which isn't boring when we are out of school'. However harmless may be the intentions of a group of young people, their existence can become a cause of tension within the community and where the local view is that the adolescent groups belong to the local school in the daytime the responsibilities incumbent upon the school are believed to be that much greater. The response from one school has been to publicly state, in a school letter to parents, that:

> stopping bullying is a responsibility of every member of the school community. Unfortunately we are unlikely to stamp it out completely but between us we can produce an environment that will not accept it and make sure that bullies are caught and punished.

This has led to consideration of the content of both the in-school curriculum and structured youth club offers to foster responsible behaviour.

Jason, mentioned in Chapter 2 (page 20), provided evidence of the value of area youth activities in 'helping you to cope with groups of people and yet making you feel that you are one of the crowd'. De Acosta (1994) suggests that progress may be made if attempts are made to reconcile the values of the school with the perceptions and expectations of the community and several of the schools within the investigation have attempted this. At one extreme, the school has worked with local governors to build on their views of what the community wants from the school, at the other the school maintains a community committee which acts as a collecting group for opinion and as a forum for balancing school and community needs. In both schools, there are advisory groups planning and developing activities through the local education authority services. These mechanisms offer a continuing link between school and parents within the community. One head commented that 'it is easier to involve the parents in something which they see as directly applicable to the life of their youngsters rather than to a more high flown set of ideas'. Another stressed the importance of the governors as a support for school policy and as representatives of the community. Several of the schools make reference to governors in public pronouncements of policy.

The development of appropriate curriculum approaches through personal and social education programmes is an aim in all the schools where staff were interviewed although the structure of the course may vary. Many pupils are slow to recognize the importance of 'PSE' or its equivalent, but 17 of the 115 interviewed consider that this type of course is a positive intervention because 'it makes you think about things', 'it helps you to cope with other people' and 'it makes it easier when you want to say no to something'. These views accord with Erwin (1995) who considers that one of the essentials for establishing a positive school climate is that all who play a part should be given training in conflict management and problem solving before becoming involved in policy development. Carter (1994) applies these essentials to gang prevention in the belief that if anti-social behaviour is tackled at school level then continuing group 'warfare' within the community may be prevented. Byrne (1994b) sees the eradication of bullying as a community responsibility and the youth service working with sample schools attempts to reinforce formal school teaching about relationships with the activities offered in two of the schools which serve neighbourhood communities. The involvement of young people in the development of community activities from the school as a safe base (Vriens 1995) has an advantage in that day school staff may be encouraged to participate alongside youth workers with enhancement of curricular and personal understanding. Three of the schools working with their communities mention the importance of the sixth form as a bridge especially where the Duke of Edinburgh Award Scheme, local football and other leagues, and school-based leisure work give opportunities for working with social groups beyond the school. Young (1994) argues that this requires all parties to maintain 'controlled assertiveness' as another skill but the resulting mutuality has been successful in improving the community culture in some areas.

Although schools make considerable efforts to work with the parents of their pupils and within the community at large, staff report a variety of tensions. Staff interviewed in five of the schools mention a gulf between the school expectations of hard work and the community view that 'it doesn't get you anywhere and it is more important to enjoy your youth because life gets tough very soon'. The instilling of a work ethic against a background of unemployment, poverty and deprivation creates a division between the pupils supported by their parents and those who do not enjoy such support except in their resistance to school. In three of the partnership schools there is reference to the lack of equal opportunities within the communities either through racism or traditional views of the role of women – again resulting in a tension between those who aspire to overcome their difficulties and those who accept them. The long history of physical retaliation as a means of settling disputes is mentioned by three schools, one of which also reports low expectations and prejudice as problems. In such an environment any attempt made by the school to eradicate violence is countered by parental support for 'getting your own back', 'giving her one' and 'not grassing'. Schwartz (1993) comments on a similar problem in Australia that 'societal and cultural attitudes towards "dobbing" [reporting] plays a major role in perpetuating the problem'. He suggests that the involvement of the community at large in positive prevention strategies may offer a way forward but this cannot begin only at secondary level and requires participation on a broader front. Consideration of the community involvement strategies suggested by Randall (1996), shows how by shared policymaking and determination a group of schools can link with the community they serve to face bullying issues, but the involvement of other social agencies requires leadership, support and funding to work with pre-school and post-school groups.

> **Reflection**   Are there dangers in a group of schools linking together for action to secure a particular aim, or to foster a particular policy? How might these be overcome?

## Schools together

There is mention in three of the case study reports of action between schools to head off problems between their members. One pupil talks about a fight between some of our pupils and those from another school who had picked on them because of a disagreement out of school . . . somehow the staff got to know and when we left school there were members of staff of both schools in the area . . . they used their radio links to prevent trouble.

Whether this was a pragmatic response to whisperings on the local network or a planned action when potential trouble was reported both schools worked together to prevent serious trouble in the area. Experience in the USA has shown that where there is a shared view of the prevention of bullying and violent behaviour amongst schools serving a community, local disturbances amongst groups are minimized. Fieldman *et al.* (1992) have charted the success of a cluster of schools serving a defined neighbourhood in the development of anti-bullying policies and their implementation through exchange of information on pupils and policies, in-service training and sharing community resources including counsellors. Having established action to meet a specified need, the cluster has now moved on to provide a forum for discussion, planning and implementation of a number of child development strategies. Importantly, the cluster has given expression to the 'cradle to grave' view of life in the community and achieved much in meeting the needs of parents and pupils at the transition periods.

We have no evidence of a cluster of schools working in such a tightly coordinated way but there are examples of joint planning of anti-bullying policies and the provision of in-service training for staff in two of the groups of schools where pupils change school at the ages of 9 and 13 years. Whilst the emphasis in this work is on continuity of values within the schools, it is also a means of alerting governors and parents to a community-wide expectation. Hazler (1994) shows that a proactive stance taken by staff in all phases of schooling prevents horse-play and teasing in the early years developing into a long-standing cause of victimization in middle years and senior school. O'Keefe (1994a) suggests that such interinstitutional planning requires additional training for the staff involved not only to ensure cohesion in the basic philosophy but also to explore the necessary changes in relationships between schools and the communities which they work with. However, Cutright (1995) argues that change cannot come from external inputs but hinges on a willingness on the part of the community. Influencing the nature of the social environment is a controlling factor in successful change. In examining the lives of black and of white children, he asserts that neighbourhood social structures may be isolated from the ethos of schools or school board planning. He suggests that successful intervention to secure improved relationships requires a system of 'measuring' the culture of communities. There is evidence that in meeting the needs of individual families the pastoral staff of schools within the sample 'have a feel for the situation and the nature of the family and community' but, as yet, none of the schools investigated have attempted to categorize the subunits within their catchment area in a more specific way. MacDougal (1993) has suggested that an audit of violence within each school district could produce the spur to action by schools within the area. She builds her views on the identification of potential bullying behaviour amongst children at the pre-nursery stage and the need for change in behaviour during the younger formative period rather than acting when bullying becomes a problem in the middle or senior years (Ziegler 1987; Williams and Schaller 1993). Community action of this sort requires continuity of knowledge and care of pupils at each stage of schooling and intervention may require the involvement of a range of agencies.

## Working with agencies in the community

Mellor (1995), in a survey of the progress of anti-bullying initiatives in Scotland, lists the agencies which are working with schools and local education authorities in 'accepting their responsibility to challenge the abuse of power wherever it happens'. Whilst the agencies range from the churches to the prison service, and from the academic community to the workplace, there is comparatively little evidence of integrated approaches to community except on a pilot basis. Amongst these initiatives is the work of the Police Research Group in the communities served by four schools in London and Liverpool. The method of working was to organize a series of anti-bullying lessons working with staff in the schools and then using community policing to support work outside school. Pitts and Smith (1996) recognize the importance of context and the development of solutions applicable to the local situation. This has been taken further by Payzant (1992) who contends that local initiatives whilst bottom-up in community involvement require support from the executives of the agencies concerned. Stone (1995) highlights the problems of fostering development at a time when agencies may be competing for scarce financial resources and when the outcomes of cooperation have still to be assessed.

There is evidence of limited interagency initiatives within the sample schools – locally with the police, probation services, social services and church organizations. One school has detailed the difficulties arising from such involvement which 'may raise expectations and does not always recognize the additional time required'. From the same school the head comments that:

> external agencies are involved but they are changing their code to a lighter touch, for example the child abuse panel has a good remit and

we know that this helps to identify those at risk but we then encounter problems of time and money and serious cases can be too big for our resources ... our governors feel that they do not want the staff to become social workers or become involved in non-disclosure disputes.

Fertman ( 1993) contrasts the legal standing of the school and the community, the former with a legal structure and clearly defined mission, the latter often with intangible aims, uncertain resourcing and differing agendas. Involvement in 'one-off, hit-and-run'-type community-improvement schemes has a limited appeal to the schools and one head sees potential problems in the willingness of governors to allow the school to become involved, but because schemes are often limited in funding and uncertain in duration the 'honey-pot' attraction may be detrimental to the community. Fertman suggests that any framework for interagency communication should involve planning based on the establishment of goals, clarity of roles, balance between participants and equality of treatment for all involved. This would give an atmosphere of trust providing that participants understand procedures in the event of conflict and have a clear idea of evaluation. Rutherford and Billig (1995) stress the importance of training for all involved in school–community initiatives, fearing that the professional superiority of teaching staff could inhibit confidence in tackling problems. This is certainly true of any local initiative which involves young people and requires an understanding of the Children Act 1989.

Failure by the community agencies to support the work of schools may result in serious anti-social behaviour. The sample schools reported only very few instances of bullying leading to expulsion but the policy in most schools is that repeated bullying will result in this sanction. The marketization of education is acting to the detriment of pupils with behavioural problems because examination success in reaching National Curriculum objectives published locally as 'league tables' or Ofsted reports detracts from the self-esteem of those pupils who do not make their mark academically and often leads to anti-social behaviour. The problem then is that placing the pupil in another school 'exports' the difficulty. Determination by some schools to 'act tough' in this situation may cause more difficulties, particularly where two or three schools are in competition within an area. Investigation of this in the USA has led to the view that there may be a degree of stereotyping of bullies which leads to solutions which have immediacy but little value for the bully who then moves from school to school. Mulhern (1994) suggests that action which fails to support bully as well as victim reinforces those elements of the bully's life which have caused his or her behaviour problem, and Cicourel (1995) argues that sanctions within the community, and linked to the juvenile justice system, may be linked to perceptions of family behaviour which allow little opportunity for progress from low levels of social achievement. Chambliss (1995) takes this argument further by suggesting that the transference of funds from education to crime control is resulting in increasingly negative community attitudes and lack of willingness to secure improvement through voluntary local action. The interview evidence resulted in many narratives of bullying activity and the consequent action which the interviewees believed was taken by the school staff. Of the 115 interviewees, 79 mentioned exclusion as a consequence of repeated or serious bullying but only three appeared to actually know youngsters who had been excluded – the problem may well exist more in the folklore than in the reality. If this is so, it can be argued that impact of schools upon the values of their communities, the support of voluntary and social agencies, and the comparatively low level of reported and actionable bullying reflect some success in the wider application of anti-bullying philosophy and practice. At the same time, our evidence suggests that minor bullying may be a source of continuing misery for some young people who 'really never go out in the evening because I am worried that there will be some trouble with the people in school who cause me problems, threaten me and leave me feeling very unsafe'.

# ⑧ CHANGING ATTITUDES

## Introduction

In the discussion so far, we have considered the practicalities of anti-bullying policies within schools. This chapter is concerned with some of the issues involved in securing changed policies within schools and the communities they serve. Successful implementation of new policies is related both to external pressures on the school and the development of new attitudes amongst the pupils, staff and community who work within the organization. To achieve change requires not only the policy but also the will to make it effective and we were concerned to see what factors ensure that the rhetoric of anti-bullying becomes a reality.

## The pressures for change

As noted in Chapter 1, the publication of the Elton report (1989) could not have come at a worse time for those who were anxious to secure a new view of disciplinary management within schools. At the time when schools should have been giving maximum attention to its content and implication, senior management were much more concerned with the issues arising from the Education Act 1988 and in particular the introduction of the National Curriculum, local management of schools and a much more open attitude to the release of detail about schools into the public arena. The intention was that parents could make choices on the basis of informed judgement and in so doing exert pressure on schools to achieve higher standards. However, these measures brought with them a readiness to consider the Elton report in the schools in a way which its authors could not have foreseen. The developments from the 1988 Act – freedom of choice of school, Ofsted and a heightened media interest in what schools were about – have all brought pressures for school improvement, one element of which is the social behaviour of pupils. This has caused pressure to be exerted on schools from a viewpoint other than that held by the Elton report. Schools were pressed to improve pupil behaviour out of a fear that they would not recruit and this led to a more draconian view of anti-social behaviour. This differs from the view that schools should develop through meeting the needs of their pupils within the school context and recognizing a responsibility extending into the community beyond their institutions.

## The open market

During the period of more open recruitment following the Education Act 1980 which had allowed a greater element of freedom for parents to express their wishes regarding their choice of school for their children, there had been a considerable body of research into the factors which might affect this choice. Adler *et al.* (1989) had shown the importance of the child's personal wish to attend a particular school matched by parental views of the discipline in schools. West and Varlaam (1991) found that this held true after the 1988 Act and Glover (1992) and others demonstrated that whilst the possible happiness of the child was a major concern, parents seeking admission to schools which they considered to have a grammar school ethos were also concerned with examination results and work emphasis. From all this work, it seems that the child's happiness is balanced against parental perceptions of 'standards'. Both of these are affected by the school's stance towards social behaviour and the way in which this is represented in the educational marketplace. The pressure for all schools to progress similarly in matters of uniform, extramural opportunities and social development is greatest where the competition is most intense. The development of organizational loyalty may intensify the views of pupils of one school about members of another and may well undermine community values. This is substantiated in the narratives from three schools within a mile of each other on the suburban fringe of one town where pupils speak in a deprecating way about their colleagues in the other schools.

Several of the sample schools, however, were spurred on by the need to improve recruitment through changing the expected pattern of behaviour of the pupils. One head commented that:

> our anti-bullying policy is fundamental because we realize that recruitment depends upon it – pupils are easily put off if they think that they will be subjected to unpleasant behaviour when they come to the school and so we have worked with the primary schools to assure them that bullying is not acceptable.

A deputy head in another school commented that:

we were aware that we were not recruiting because the parents were asked why they did not send their youngsters to us, and their reply that bullying seemed to be a problem led to some reconsideration and making public what we knew we already did.

In the second school, 'everyone has the right to education without being frightened and this is a big step from the days when changing schools was associated with intimidation and ill-treatment'. Recruitment is less of an overt driving force for change in the remaining sample schools. Of these, six have a statement of values which provide a framework for 'equality of opportunity', 'a fair deal', 'freedom to make the most of all opportunities', 'honesty and responsibility for actions' and a school which is 'strong on relationships'. In five schools, there are no widely known policy state-ments but evidence shows that staff of the schools believe in the import-ance of 'caring', 'relationships', 'knowing that we won't tolerate any bullying' and 'providing for maximum achievement' and transmit these ideals to many of the pupils. In the remaining three schools, although there is evidence that policies are being developed, there is no consistency in staff attitude shown at its worst in the comments of a standard scale teacher that 'I don't know of any policy but we do what we think is neces-sary to cope with the situation at the time' which conflicts with a deputy head view that 'we have a strong view of what we ought to be doing to prevent bullying'. In these schools other pressures for change appear to be more important than the need to use enhanced pupil relationships as a means of sustaining recruitment. Two are schools with a clear neighbour-hood catchment and considerable socio-economic difficulty and the third is a school in a rural town which has no competition from other schools in the maintained sector.

Although the existence of an anti-bullying policy may be known, printed in the brochures and publicity material about a school, and made much of at the recruitment stage, Hammond and Dennison (1995) have shown that the reality of choice is dependent upon parental ability to pay for transport to another school. With this is linked the 'hidden costs' of uniform and activities at another school. If this is so, it might be considered that schools where, because of socio-economic factors, very few parents might be exercising choice do not give such a high priority as others to developing a clear anti-bullying policy. Of the 18 schools in the sample, the most clearly expressed policies are in those schools where the interschool competition is strongest (e.g. where two or three schools serve a compara-tively affluent urban area), where transport is provided within a common area and where schools are attempting to attract pupils from a wider and undefined catchment. Whilst anti-bullying policies appear to be more explicit in those schools which face competition, this does not negate the efforts made in other schools to establish a caring community. The deputy head of one of the sample schools interprets any anti-social behaviour seriously 'without making undue reference to bullying' and there is clear evidence that the staff use a consistent and known policy for all aspects of anti-social behaviour without differentiating between aspects of bullying or any other behaviour which upsets others. Significantly, the pupil narratives from this school are concerned with 'smokers', 'the gangs' and those who 'muck about so that we can't get on with our lessons' and few pupil interviewees made any reference to specific bullying.

### Ofsted reporting

Whilst anti-bullying policies may be important in reaching the potential pupils within an area, senior staff who were interviewed felt that comparatively few parents define their needs and seek reassurances before making a decision about a school, although hearsay evidence from our sample of schools indicates that there is now a greater willingness by parents from all social groups to become involved in the transfer process. The development of pupil contracts as a means of securing parental cooperation with the school may well enhance this involvement. Increasingly more significant is the availability of Ofsted reports. In many instances, these have been selectively reported to the public by the staff of the school or by the local press but the importance of securing a favourable report to ensure a continuing local reputation has led some schools to consider issues of behaviour. Of the 18 schools where staff were interviewed three were motivated to reconsider and rewrite their policies about behaviour because of an impending inspection. Others 'tidied up the policy as we got everything ready for the inspection', 'reviewed everything that moved within the school and went for all aspects of care and the pastoral policy', 'set out the way in which the aims of the school were translated into the realities of everyday life' and 'attempted to bring about some degree of consistency between what we did in each year group'.

---

**Reflection**   Does the Ofsted process increase the likelihood of the development of ineffective policies?

---

In so far as the aim of the inspection process is to bring about sustained school improvement, consideration of strategies for change and the development of monitoring and evaluation (Davis 1996), any attempts to bring about a policy framework and to secure its implementation would appear advantageous. To this end, the Ofsted reports for those schools which have already been inspected, and which have given full data to the current investigation were compared. Thirteen schools have had their reports published and eight reports make some reference to aspects of pupil relationships including the existence of an anti-bullying policy. This is commended where it shows elements of the management of communication of the principles and practice, consistency in application and the processes and use of monitoring. For example in one report:

> The school has a written policy against bullying, which is well documented and operates efficiently. There are clear strategies for its implementation and in the few instances where it has needed to operate, Heads of Year have provided appropriate monitoring arrangements.

In common with the development of the rational model for review, planning and implementation (Glover *et al.* 1996) of all aspects of effective school management the need for monitoring is mentioned in two other reports, and the need for consistency in a further two where 'it is important that the recording of incidents and their causes are carefully monitored to ensure that the policy is being implemented consistently and effectively'.

There is no reference to bullying, either as behaviour, or as a reason for policy development in the reports on five schools. In these, there is reference in more inclusive terms to relationships which 'are mainly good and often excellent', and to 'clear expectations for standards of behaviour and discipline which are fully understood by the whole school community'. In one report, there is no overt reference to the management of bullying but the message is clear in the comment that the school 'mirrors the community it serves ... long-standing family antagonisms are sometimes brought into school and have led to fighting and injury'. Whether Ofsted has been a catalyst for change or merely a spur for systematization and communication of practice within schools (Brimblecombe *et al.* 1996) interview evidence shows that monitoring and evaluation of the implemented policy only occurs in a small proportion of schools – three in the sample of eighteen. It is likely that action plans arising from comment in reports will secure more coherent and consistent policies as schools reconsider their behaviour management. For example:

> The school is aware of the possibility of bullying and it is dealt with in the curriculum in KS4. Staff are invited in the staff brochure to refer to the school's bullying policy, but it does not appear in the list of policy statements available for reference in the staff library. Further steps should be taken to ensure that all members of staff are fully aware of the policy and that such issues are raised with pupils earlier in their school career.

## Media interest

Bullying stories have become the stuff of the tabloid press in recent years and the all too frequent suicide attempts have brought the issue to the attention of a public which, whilst remembering the apparent horrors of its own childhood, is seeking to ensure that the coming generation is able to handle such pressures. Kenny (1995), in response to an account of an adolescent suicide, asks 'whatever happened to the stiff upper lip?' but by far the greater pressure is for the development of a society within which bullying would not be acceptable behaviour. The use of narratives based upon the suffering of the victims is increasingly being used to bring about a change of attitude as shown by Marano (1995), in a popular press article summarizing the impact of bullying and Maynard (1993) draws from the research to suggest strategies for parents to help them support children at risk.

The public interest is only a factor in changed attitudes if it can be marshalled in some way. This is at the heart of current media support for Frances Lawrence in her campaign for greater moral awareness and in the work of the Schools Curriculum and Assessment Authority in seeking an enhanced moral content in the national curriculum (*The Guardian*, 1 January 1997). Marston (1996) describes the way in which some change has been achieved through the work of the National Confederation of Parent-Teacher Associations bringing a concern that over 40 per cent of schools do not have active anti-bullying policies. As a pressure group with representation in 11 000 schools, this may bring considerable pressure to bear on national policy development, reflected to some extent in the current concern that spiritual, moral and cultural education should be given greater prominence in schools, and also affect the attitudes of governors as policymakers in the schools. Of the eighteen schools in which heads were interviewed, five spoke of aspects of the 'need to address a national issue and to establish a response to school requirements' and three mention that 'the current concerns have arisen from media interest – especially at the local level' and combined with recruitment pressures unwelcome publicity for any incident could be detrimental. The schools in one local education authority divisional area covered in the Keele Partnership investigation have also been involved in a parallel drive to improve attendance and local media attention to the link between bullying and truancy (Carlen *et al*. 1992). This has highlighted the importance of making parents aware of their responsibilities to secure attendance whilst assuring them of security for pupils within the school. The existence of a policy alone is not a sufficient safeguard and our investigation has shown that implementation requires a much broader acceptance of a set of principles of social behaviour than Ofsted reports indicate some schools are able to achieve.

## The process of change

The variety of motives for the introduction of anti-bullying policies has already been investigated in Chapter 5 but the way in which change is successfully achieved owes much to the understanding of organizational behaviour on the part of senior management in schools. New policies 'hastily cobbled together to meet the needs of a forthcoming Ofsted inspection' or 'put out for the staff as a guide to show how we would be dealing with bullying in the future', appear to have been unsuccessful as judged by the mismatch between intention and pupil experience in two of the schools in our sample. Successful intervention has occurred where the new policy is driven by a will on the part of both staff and pupils to achieve a better society. In seven schools, the discussion has been opened up with parents and governors have also been active rather than receptors of a policy presented to them by the senior staff of the school. By contrast, in another seven schools the policy is variable in content and interpretation across the year groups and has arisen from attempts made by 'missioner individuals' to change the nature of relationships. Beare *et al.* (1989) demonstrate the importance of a shared vision of what any change is intended to achieve and Stott and Walker (1992) stress the need for common understanding by all parties of the intent of any mission or values statement. Comments from the staff in these schools indicate that whilst individually they are working for improved relationships between pupils, there is little evidence that this is part of a coherent policy.

Fullan (1991) argues that change which is institution-wide needs to grow from properly planned and resourced professional development linked to school-improvement planning. In the schools under review, approaches to anti-bullying training vary considerably. In some, policies have been developed after a period of time in which issues, introduced at a one-day staff conference, have been discussed by staff at department and year level. In others, working parties have been established after the topic has been introduced, and in five schools the group which dealt with innovation has continued to function as a monitoring group. The nature of the training day has varied but interview evidence suggests that staff have been introduced to the realities of bullying behaviour, its implications for individual and school development and alternative strategies for intervention.

Mellor (1995) details three types of training which are needed within schools – awareness raising, anti-bullying strategy training and information giving either generally or to targeted groups. He argues that most training to date has been of the awareness raising type but that strategy development has been more slowly implemented, especially where only a few staff have been given the task of achieving change.

Galloway (1994) considers that fundamental changes of attitude may need to grow from training which is concerned with principles rather than with simply awareness-raising. He concludes that issues such as the facilitation of detection, open speaking, participative decision-making, developing self-esteem and ongoing evaluation may actually require more fundamental changes of attitude than can be accommodated in a one-day course. There are examples of 'how to' types of training materials such as those offered by the Commission for Racial Equality or Kidscape but unless these are an aid to policy development rather than simply introducing tactical help, they may have a limited value. McNamara (1995) urges 'evolution not intervention' and this element of continuing activity is seen by pupils who, both in the open comment and in interviews suggested that the reiteration of policies was necessary if anti-bullying approaches are to have a long-term effect. One year head commented that 'where there has been a degree of success in past anti-bullying campaigns there are comparatively few instances of overt bullying and as a result the policy can get forgotten'. To a Year 11 pupil, however, this is seen as:

> going along without saying anything much about what would happen if there was to be any bullying and then when there is an incident going ape in the way they [the staff] act, so that you get fed up with what has happened without realizing what the deeper things are all about.

Surprisingly, there is little evidence that staff are aware of the implications of the Children Act which although setting parameters for the involvement of all social agencies in dealing with pupils with problems, has not been used as a focus of training within schools. To one head it is 'used negatively, when we could make much more of it as a positive framework to support changed attitudes amongst staff'.

The pattern of a training day at Thames High School is offered as an example of the approach to heightened staff interest in policy development. It follows a survey of pupil perceptions and initial discussions as staff in the lower school of a large 11–18 comprehensive attempted to meet pupil concerns. It is offered as a catalyst for longer-term change applicable to one school given its context at that time and was developed to overcome resistance to change from some members of staff who did not feel that bullying presented any problems within the school.

Whilst the importance of staff training as an element in the management of change has been stressed Rutherford and Billig (1995) argue that appropriate and simultaneous training for parents, governors and community is an essential for major policy change. Above all, pupil training is crucial for success otherwise they will feel that they are 'being done to' rather than helped by developments.

**Thames High School, Training Day 1995**

*9.00–9.30  Training of 7–10 group leaders*

*9.30  Course leader*

Explain style. Confidentiality. Safety. Relaxed. Positive about
ourselves and each other. Explain purpose of the group. Twofold:
1  To look at whole school approaches. Work done at Greendale
   High School. The next steps at Thames High in the light of their
   survey report , pupils' and working party suggestions.
2  Dealing with bullying incidents. Increasing confidence and
   expertise when dealing with bullying. This will involve:
   (a)  looking at our own experience, thoughts and feelings about
        bullying, bullies, victims and survivors of bullying;
   (b)  discussing strategies for dealing with specific incidents.

*9.45  Dealing with incidents*

Look at *Thames High definition of bullying. In pairs each person take a
turn* to tell partner of any time when s/he was mistreated in any of
those ways. Describe in detail the earliest incident you can
remember including who, what, when and where. When it's your
turn to listen give good attention and don't interrupt with your
story. Encourage your partner to describe her feelings especially
towards the perpetrator(s). Finish by considering how well you did
despite the circumstances and give an explanation for the bullying
behaviour that was to do with them rather than you.

*9.55  Brainstorm* the explanations for the behaviour on to the
overhead projector.

*10.00  In same pair take a turn* telling partner of any time you have
done any of the above to anyone else. How did you feel during and
afterwards? What was the explanation for your behaviour?

Add the explanations to the OHP.

Short talk on re-stimulation of hurtful memories and how our
feelings confuse us when we are faced with a bullying incident.

*10.20  Basic principles of assertiveness on OHP*

*10.25 In fours discuss incidents* which you have witnessed in school where someone was mistreated in any of those ways. Write down your responses on a large sheet. Give them to anti-bullying working party members for display.

*Anti-bullying working party members display strategies on the walls*

*10.45 Whole school approaches.* Leader explains what they have been doing at Greendale. Look at Greendale's anti-bullying policy.

*10.55 Break*

*11.15 Divide into groups of 10 and go to rooms* (best in departments or year groups and non-teachers in their own groups). Each group will be led by a member of the anti-bullying working party.

*11.20 Read* the results of the *lower school questionnaire and suggestions for action* from the pupils. Also look at Thames High's *procedures for dealing with bullies,* the *ideas of the anti-bullying working party* and *their report to the governors* and the sheets entitled *'Why an anti-bullying policy?'*

*11.35 Group's written recommendations.* As a group discuss the ideas on these sheets and your own. Write down the group's ideas and recommendations for formulating a whole school policy on bullying. *These will be forwarded to the headteacher and the anti-bullying working party* to be collated into a written policy.

*11.55 Group decide what idea they want the leader to highlight in the plenary session. Finish session.*

*12.00 Plenary session. Each group leader to highlight their group's strongest idea.*

---

**Reflection**    Consider the *Thames High School* programme for the training day and analyse the new concepts which the staff are likely to have to accept. What follow-up work with the whole staff, groups and individuals might be necessary?

## Perceptions and problems

Anti-bullying is but one of many initiatives which require the time and attention of teaching staff who are frequently resistant to whole-school policy evolution. For most, this discussion is taking place at a time when most subject areas are undergoing change in order to meet the requirements of National Curriculum implementation and this appears to create an order of priorities which inhibits whole school change. In this situation, Frank and Rocks (1996) suggest that the four components of organizational change – conceptualization, communication, commitment and control – are of fundamental importance. They seek: a clear aim and a belief that nothing would be undertaken unless it was a necessary prerequisite to improvement; that the idea and all the steps in its implementation should be clearly communicated to all participants with an opportunity for feedback; that the commitment of the majority of participants should be elicited at a very early stage with a frank discussion and recognition of all obstacles to change; and that organizational changes should be made so that success is maintained (e.g. through the greater availability of resources). Evidence from two schools indicates that 'off-the-cuff' policies offered to the staff without necessary support have been failures. Successful change requires consideration of several aspects of school management.

### Staff attitudes

Mention has already been made of the varying interpretations of the word 'bullying' and its connotations for all members of the school. Interview evidence indicates that many of the teaching staff of the sample schools feel that 'there is too much attention to bullying and we had very little difficulty until media and the governors started asking questions'. A year head in a school in which pupils and some staff recognize that bullying is a problem comments that:

> the school ethos accepts verbal bullying . . . you hear it as you walk around and teachers don't think that they are behaving in a way which is other than acceptable to the youngsters . . . as a result pupils find it difficult to reconcile the stated policy and the behaviours they see around them and because all incidents are dealt with in an individualized way the policy issues aren't faced, but nobody would say that there is a bullying atmosphere.

In the same set of interviews, the head comments upon the raised expectations because of local media interest and suggests that there may be a degree of unreality in the wider interpretation of the term. One of the staff sees this as 'the more parents and children are aware of the problems the more they look for them'.

Even where there is an 'official' line which includes a definition of bullying as shown in policy materials and on classroom posters, reactionary
behaviours may persist amongst some staff. One head comments that:

> it is not just a matter of the staff not realizing how grave a problem we
> have ... we don't want to start alarmist stories within the area, it is
> also a matter of getting them to look at their own way of relating to
> other people.

A female member of staff in one school, formerly a boys' grammar school,
argues that 'there is a continuation of old attitudes and sexual innuendo
and misplaced humour of some colleagues is a problem here' whilst
another woman main scale teacher says that 'there is implicit bullying of
staff by some of the senior management although they may not realize that
they are doing it and women are especially vulnerable'. The need for clear
guidelines and total involvement in consideration of staff attitudes is
reflected in the professional concern that, with a harder management
stance in many schools, approaches which could be interpreted as bullying affect staff who then adopt harder attitudes to pupils (Marston 1996).

Staff attitudes to pupils are also interpreted with a bullying component
by the pupils. Of the 115 interviewed, 46 refer to the 'shouting by the
teachers' and 27 refer to 'teachers not knowing what is going on'. In
answering the questionnaire, 10 per cent of the pupils made additional
open comments. Of these 489 responses, 24 per cent are sceptical of teacher
intervention, whilst 13 per cent of the cohort answering the questionnaire
are positive about the efforts of the schools and the teachers to ensure a
safe and secure environment for the pupils. Nine pupils making open
comments say that they would not have the courage to tell a teacher and a
further seven either would not or could not do so for other reasons. These
reasons emerging at other places in the comment are related to staff failure
to understand what is going on, failure to listen to what pupils are saying
to them, likelihood that they would not support victims and a fear that
they would over-react to the situation.

All staff are faced with difficulties in handling bullying. One head comments that 'they have their own attitudes which are caught up with their
memories of what happened in their own school experience and do not
consider anything to be serious if it is beyond direct physical bullying'.
Certainly the view of one deputy that 'the whole thing is out of proportion,
bullying is a buzz word and becomes the excuse for any failure in relationships' is mirrored in the comments that pupils make of the effectiveness of
staff intervention. In five of the eighteen schools where staff were interviewed, senior managers speak of the slow change of attitude where some
staff either do not recognize bullying or else accept that this is part of the
pattern of growing up, and this is especially so in the three schools where
parental attitudes are more likely to favour retaliatory behaviour. Table 8.1

**Table 8.1** Pupil perception of staff taking mistreatment 'very seriously'

| Behaviour | Percentage |
|---|---|
| Racism taunts | 56 |
| Gender issues | 16 |
| Learning difficulties ridiculed | 55 |
| Religious background criticized | 37 |
| Hard work criticized | 21 |

summarizes pupils' perception of the effectiveness of interventions to meet certain types of bullying.

Despite the pupil view of limited teacher effectiveness, interview evidence leads us to believe that in some of the schools considerable efforts are being made to support both teaching staff and non-teaching staff in the development of a more positive society. These include the production of materials for assemblies, form or tutor periods and personal and social education. However, one pupil has interpreted this as 'having worksheets to do when I would rather talk through the issues' and another as 'being given things to do from worksheets whilst the teacher is doing other things and this doesn't help us to work things out'. The time needed for investigation, counselling and monitoring of any incidents is seen by some teachers to 'be out of proportion to the seriousness of what has occurred', 'to involve crisis intervention at a time of day when we have other pressures' and 'to open an issue which may be a local can of worms ... we aren't social workers'. One head felt that the only way in which staff could be persuaded to undertake anti-bullying with a degree of commitment was if 'it could change the relationships between the youngsters in such a way that we would not have the problems in the future'. Unfortunately, pupil attitudes are also slow to change.

## Pupil attitudes

Whatever efforts are made by the staff of schools children bring with them the values of the home when they come to school and much of the evidence in earlier chapters reflects this. At one extreme, some pupils have a deep sense of prejudice against racial groups, the affluent or disadvantaged, and those with disability. At the other extreme, there may be no overt prejudice but rather a clash of personalities which cannot be rationalized. This is especially marked in areas of socio-economic deprivation such as some of the housing estates in the current investigation where levels of unemployment and consequent poverty are high, where family groups are defensive and where there is a tension between the values of home and school. Erwin (1995) suggests that pupils from this type of environment have low interpersonal relationship skills and resort to violence as a defence but recognizes that intervention at the secondary stage may be too late and that interagency work with families from pre-school may be a necessary prerequisite for improved social interaction at the secondary level. Whether prejudice is a reflection of attitudes at home or of former interfamily tensions the school is frequently seen to be exceeding its proper role, which one pupil summed up as 'teaching us the subjects and letting us get on with our own problems'. This is a possible explanation for the pupil perception that only 26 per cent would tell their form tutor and 22 per cent their year tutor if they were being physically mistreated. These figures are explained in interview evidence which shows a reluctance to tell because of a fear of 'getting done for grassing' and it does seem that in some of the schools the intention to achieve a new set of relationships manifest in 'anti-bullying charter', 'fair deal' or 'opportunity for all' is negated by pupil unwillingness to expose troublemakers. This is partly related to immaturity in knowing what type of event should be reported, partly to a fear of reprisals summed up as 'making it worse for yourself by dobbing', and partly to a lack of confidence in the way in which teachers would handle the incident and maintain confidentiality. Hoover and Juul (1993) highlight the importance of spotting behaviour traits which might indicate individual or group unhappiness but the narratives disclosed by some of the interviewees indicate considerable skill shown by adolescents in masking inner feelings. To one girl there 'is no need to let the teachers know what is happening because it only means more questions and the pressure is on'.

Three groups of young people are particularly vulnerable and interviews and open comment show that racial, sexual and verbal unkindness, especially to the least able, are frequent causes of distress. The change of attitude needed to secure a better school experience for all pupils requires recognition of the strengths of diversity and much PSE work has this as an aim. However, whilst 6 per cent of the questionnaire respondents admit that they have discriminated against others because of race, 7 per cent because of gender, and 6 per cent because of learning disabilities a greater proportion of pupils discriminate because of hard work (8 per cent) and being clever (13 per cent). This reflects a recurrent theme in current antisocial behaviour analysis that the work ethic is frowned upon by many adolescents and especially by the boys. This may be a reaction by some underachievers who because they cannot succeed determine to inhibit the progress of others. This is seen in the comment that:

> some kids do well and they get praised in class but I have never been like that and I know that the other kids like me because I am good for

a laugh and it doesn't really make much difference because there won't be a job when I finish anyway.

The Ofsted reports for the schools in the survey indicate that efforts are being made through equal opportunities policies and special needs practice to instil positive attitudes towards others. One school is commended as follows:

> The school has a strong and detailed anti-racism policy and there is a commitment to equality of opportunity in its statement of values document. The governors' policy statement on equal opportunities has been published in the school newsletter and parents have been encouraged to support it. The school seeks to involve pupils of all races in school life ... The effect of the anti-racism policy is being properly monitored with incidents being formally recorded.

The report of another school shows the philosophical basis accepted by all staff and developed with the pupils:

> The school aims to exercise teaching methods which are sensitive to the needs of the individual policy and which are non-discriminatory ... the special needs policy states that each child is of equal value and that there should be equal opportunities for all pupils to fulfil their social and academic potential.

Where such policies are maintained, harassment may be minimized because of a sustained aim to develop positive pupil attitudes. The evidence from pupils suggests that anti-bullying is seen as a separate issue and it may be that the two schools which have a coherent and integrated behaviour policy but no anti-bullying policy may be working from a more general philosophical stance. Integrationist policies are supported by Chazan et al. (1994), in looking at the problems likely to be encountered by those pupils with behavioural difficulties and Thompson et al. (1994b) support this view but would encourage some special arrangements such as the availability of support staff and of refuge areas to minimize exposure to potentially adverse groups of mainstream pupils. There is evidence that the 'hardened' bully, aware of the sanctions system of the school will use his, or her, provocative tendencies in anti-social behaviour which will result in temporary exclusion. Local political pressure is for these youngsters to be contained within the school but the intensity of market forces is such that some schools see immediacy of exclusion as a way of informing the community of their values.

Shakeshaft (1995), having identified sexual harassment as a particular problem for girls viewed as unattractive dressers, overdeveloped girls and non-macho boys, suggests that staff need to be aware of 'at-risk' pupils and that strategies which involve working with pupil and peers in small groups may be necessary for enhanced pupil understanding of the value of each individual. Stein (1995) believes that whole-school policies based upon the worth of each individual and firm action against any known infringement of personal esteem and 'space' might reduce sexual harassment. Some of this work is outlined in Chapter 9. However, although behaviour in front of staff may be good, that which develops away from adult supervision requires a greater level of pupil self-control than may be possible in the early secondary years.

In all these situations, changed attitudes depend upon two formative influences. The first is a greater level of understanding of individual differences which Quicke (1995) argues would grow from a more democratic interpupil discourse building on the strengths of pupils' cultural environment – open discussion of issues enhances the ability of pupils to defend their position and 'say no' without fear of retaliation. The second influence is that of the home and the encouragement of common support for positive action from school and parents. One of the schools in the sample is commended for the involvement of parents in homework supervision and on the 'expectations' and 'equal opportunities' working groups. The problem is that 'the pupils who most need their parents to be involved are those who have least to do with us'.

Where pupil and staff attitudes reinforce a positive stance in general policies such as equal opportunities and behaviour there appears to be a greater chance of success for those policies which are seen as the detail for the achievement of the larger aims of the school. This is reflected in the series of comments in one report that:

> The behaviour of pupils is very good. The school is a very orderly community; pupils move around the school in a sensible way; the number of exclusions is low.
> The extensive programme of work against bullying is effective . . .
> The school's aims include some explicit reference to equal opportunities. There is significant evidence of high profile activity in this area.

By contrast, in a school where the policies are fragmentary both in design and implementation:

> A number of initiatives have positive effects on pupils' skills and confidence, but do not reach all the pupils most in need and neither self-awareness nor self-esteem is sufficiently developed in the daily life of the school. There is lack of respect in the daily life of the school for some teachers and for some pupils.
> There is some concern among parents about indiscipline at the school . . .

This raises questions about the culture of the school and the relationship between this and the effectiveness of anti-bullying policies. In Chapter 9 we present three case studies of schools which are moving along a line of progression from a pragmatic approach to the crisis management of anti-social behaviour to an approach based upon cultural modification through curriculum development.

**Reflection**    How far do media influences affect pupil attitudes towards relationships? Is there a potential for a clash of cultures between school and pupil expectations of acceptable behaviour?

# 9 THEY DID IT THIS WAY

## Introduction

So far we have discussed the management of change as illustrated in secondary schools which have progressed along different paths to implement anti-bullying policies for their pupils. This chapter will present three case studies which demonstrate in some detail how such policies have been introduced and put into practice. It will examine the principles and aims behind the policies; the successes and problems that have arisen; and the ways these are monitored. The schools have been selected as examples moving along a continuum of change which involves the acceptance of shared values, understanding of the policy for intervention, and management of individual, group and social needs. Their position on the continuum is determined by how long the policy has been pursued and the extent of its effectiveness as indicated by data from the survey, pupils' written comments, and staff and pupil interviews.

## Case study schools

### Oakley High School

Oakley High School typifies those at the beginning of the continuum where policies have been introduced in the last few years, but as yet there still appears to be a high proportion of bullies and victims compared to the other partnership schools. It has the highest percentage of pupils reporting being victims of physical bullying and the fifth highest of pupils reporting being bullies. The anti-bullying policy is part of a behaviour code introduced in 1994 and is developed through a very successful pastoral programme. The pupils interviewed are on the whole convinced of the value it places on relationships. The staff refer to a high level of deprivation in what is a predominantly working-class school and within a 'neutral' atmosphere they are united and committed in their approach to the issues.

### Downlands High School

Downlands High School, a larger establishment but with a similar social class intake, is an example of a school further along the continuum. An anti-bullying policy was adopted in 1993 in response to rising problems in an 'adverse' atmosphere. It has the third highest percentage of physically bullied and sixth highest percentage of physical bullies. The policy clearly outlines procedures and strategies, the majority of staff appear to understand the issues and share its values, and pupils are now more willing to report incidents. The major problem seems to be a mismatch of school and community values regarding bullying.

### Greendale High School

Greendale High School is one of the earliest schools in our sample to initiate its policy and as such is furthest along the continuum. It is the largest of the schools surveyed and has a mostly middle-class intake. A 'positive' atmosphere has been conducive to its anti-bullying policy which began in 1990. Various indicators suggest there has been a reduction in bullying and raising of security with the severity and frequency of physical and property bullying being relatively low. Nevertheless, like other schools which have been raising awareness of bullying over some time, the percentage of pupils reporting occasional verbal, physical and property bullying is a little over the norm. Both staff and pupil interviews show a high awareness of anti-bullying work and support for the policy.

### Oakley High School

This small mixed comprehensive school is located on a pleasant and extensive campus on the edge of a medium-sized town. Relatively few of its 500 11–16-year olds are from the immediate vicinity and most come from a large council housing estate. There are 32 teachers and the average size class is 20 pupils. There is high unemployment with above average deprivation and about 26 per cent of pupils receiving free school meals. There is a whole range of ability with a preponderance of below average ability. Less than 2 per cent of pupils come from ethnic minority heritages. It has a reputation for being a well-ordered, unassuming school with a caring ethos led well with high-quality staff. The school is very strong pastorally with a morally weighted PSE programme. Although the amount of occasional bullying is average for the sample, those who reported frequent bullying is relatively higher, especially physical bully-ing which has the highest percentage (12 per cent compared to the norm of 6 per cent) of the 25 schools. Frequent verbal and property bullying is slightly higher than average. 145 pupils were surveyed with 15 written responses (9.9 per cent of the cohort) and five teachers and seven pupils were interviewed.

### Establishing a policy

The deputy headteacher explains: 'We don't have an anti-bullying policy as such, rather a code of conduct linked with proactive and assertive discipline.' This 'Code of Behaviour' is 'a positive rather than a negative approach to anti-bullying' to address the need for 'improved behaviour which is important to lessons and improved learning'. It is for this reason that anti-bullying is an unwritten part of the overall behaviour code which is the 'spine of the school and something we continually come back to'. It is reinforced at form time and in assemblies with a copy in every classroom and at the beginning of every pupil's day book. There is purposely no specific mention of bullying behaviour in the 'Code of Behaviour' though it is mentioned in the second page of the pupils' day book.

---

**Oakley High School**

CODE OF BEHAVIOUR

The two rules for all of us at Oakley are:
(a) Everyone will act with courtesy and consideration to others at all times.
(b) Everyone must respect the environment within which we work.

This means that:
1  You should always try to respect other people's point of view.
2  In class you should make it as easy as possible for everyone to learn and for the teacher to teach.
3  You move gently and quietly about the school.
4  You always speak politely to everyone and use a low voice.
5  You are quiet whenever you are required to be.
6  You keep the school clean and tidy so that it is a welcoming place we can all be proud of.
7  You are smartly dressed in proper school uniform.

---

**Oakley High School**

GETTING IT RIGHT IN THE CLASSROOM

1 Arrive on time with everything you need for the lesson.
2 Listen to and follow instructions, first time.
3 Keep hands, feet and objects to yourself.
4 No swearing or name-calling.
5 Let other people work without interruption.

---

All the staff interviewed see the code as encouraging respect for others and the environment thereby underpinning everything done in school. This theme is key in their PSE programme, forming a main module in Year 7 and being reinforced in all years of the school. A strong pastoral team has the heads of years working closely with the form tutors who remain with their groups from Year 8 to Year 11, monitoring any bullying incidents and taking 'appropriate action'. Being a small school facilitates daily briefings which improve communication and awareness.

**Policy into practice**

The 1994 Ofsted report notes that the aims defined in the newly intro-duced behaviour code are being consistently encouraged daily by all staff members and the report specifically comments on 'good behaviour and courtesy of the pupils among themselves and with staff and visitors con-stantly in evidence both within and outside the classroom'. The report praises the 'clearly defined pastoral system' which 'particularly helps those pupils whose home backgrounds are less supportive of the school's intentions'. According to the pre-Ofsted inspection survey, the number of actively involved parents is small, but as a whole they strongly support the school's approach and are very positive about its policies and prac-tice.

Apart from being implicit within the two documents reproduced above there is no written anti-bullying policy or structure for action. The Ofsted report refers to 'the school's policy to combat bullying [which] reinforces positive relationships through a programme in PSE and has been success-ful in minimising its incidence'. Through this unwritten policy, form tutors support pupils through what one tutor calls 'a strong ladder of communi-cation to head and governors'. However, she adds that 'problems are headed off before they get to the head and governors if at all possible'. According to one head of department there is an 'awareness of the pastoral and PSE programme. All staff and pupils know it will be dealt with and investigated. We take bullying seriously. When bullying is raised by pupils the school doesn't duck it.'

A head of year refers to two specific strategies that 'are interlinked or part of a common policy. The first is via form and year activities, in PSE with bullying as a specific topic. The second is dealing with cases.' He draws attention to the fine balance kept between active and passive promotion of strategies: 'We don't just wait for pupils to tell us whether they are being bullied and we don't go looking for bullies.' Instead they monitor bullying through pastoral, PSE, form tutoring and other activities, 'where we do notice what is going on'. However, he emphasizes that monitoring bullying behaviour is just part of a larger process: 'Other behaviour problems are more pressing and bullying is not a big issue in this school, though it goes on.'

To enable teachers to become aware of bullying behaviour, pupils are encouraged to form positive relationships and to be open about their experiences with each other and their teachers. When asked how the aims of the school determine policy regarding pupil relationships, a senior teacher reiterates that 'we try hard not to call our policy an anti-bullying policy project and call it a code of behaviour to incorporate a broad approach which involves respect for persons'. The code is 'linked with investment in the school's pastoral team as our pupils come from often disadvantaged backgrounds. The team work well together with a lot of front loading in Year 7.' A tutor new to the school appreciates this approach: 'The pastoral team work well together and there is support. When I came here I was inducted well and communication with the pastoral team is well established.' Another tutor confirmed this. 'By investing in monitoring and dealing with bullying in Year 7 the policy pays dividends in reducing bullying in the upper school.'

The policy relies strongly on the awareness and sensitivity of form tutors whom the senior teacher says have 'a high profile vis-à-vis school policy on codes of behaviour'. She points out: 'Anti-bullying has to be seen in the context of this school policy and ethos. There is a school awareness over time of the link between bullying and anti-social behaviour.' This strong investment in the pastoral curriculum includes promoting enough freedom and safety for pupils to disclose bullying incidences. A head of year says they encourage pupils to talk 'to help both the bully and the bullied' and the Ofsted report refers to personal counselling provided by the deputy head and heads of year which is provided with 'sensitivity and care' both for difficulties relating to school work and for personal problems. It also points out that 'care is taken to inform the form tutor and wherever possible they are involved in the work'.

However, form tutors have other curricular demands on their time and this is taken into account by one of the year heads: 'We encourage all staff to be involved and INSET is important in this. We also try to marry subject

priorities with pastoral issues but people have other demands.' Nevertheless, the importance of having relationship issues incorporated across the
curriculum, is stressed by the senior teacher:

> Policy is linked with raising standards of behaviour, achievement and
> motivation. The curriculum allows this in relationships in RE, Eng-
> lish, and humanities, equal opportunities, anti-racism, gender, etc.
> which are all part of the code of behaviour. Issues to do with behav-
> iour, relations between pupils and staff, pastoral issues, and INSET
> issues are seen to be interlinked with raising standards of behaviour,
> achievement and motivation.

## Monitoring

There are formal methods of monitoring bullying incidences alongside
other behaviour issues, though the records are not collated systematically
as a formal quantitative measure. No bullying surveys were mentioned
apart from the Keele Partnership project. The deputy headteacher explains
the process as follows:

> We monitor through logs, pastoral team discussions and with year
> tutors. The pastoral team meets every week and looks at logs and
> reports. It involves five heads of year and the deputy head of pastoral
> as well as the pupils concerned. We are insistent and investigate but
> keep this at a low profile and follow up on the bully and the bullied.
> Most monitoring at this meeting is not to do with bullying but other
> issues. We have about seven or eight serious cases of bullying a year
> and that could involve one individual.

This form of monitoring is used and familiar to all regardless of seniority. For example a Year 7 tutor says: 'We log all cases and incidences but
these are not used in a statistical way but in terms of what staff know and
feel about them.' A senior teacher likewise refers to the school having

> no formal system of evaluation but we rely on forward investment
> and the pastoral year system. It is difficult to measure as inputs are via
> PSE, form and year tutors. Monitoring is through individual cases
> and diaries. These observable cases are easy to deal with because you
> can see it. *In extremis* it involves suspension but this is very unusual.
> Our investment in Year 7 heads off so many later problems.

Ofsted reports favourably on this approach and the sensible criteria for
exclusion which related only to incidents of severe anti-social behaviour.
The Year 7 tutor voices a common opinion expressed by staff at all levels
that 'bullying is unusual in this school'. Similarly, a Year 8 tutor believes:

The school is very effective in monitoring and dealing with behaviour problems via heads of year and form tutors. These cases are registered, logged and followed up. Bullying is not usually the priority issue.

The head of Year 9 sums up this confidence in a monitoring system which is 'a combination of "feel" of staff and case files on particular pupils'.

## Successes

The two main aspects of the policy, encouraging good relationships and the reporting procedures for when they break down, although not written as such, seem known to most of the pupils interviewed. They all reveal how important relationships and being friends with others are and most refer to the friendliness of the teachers. Five of them mention relationships as being part of the policy and refer to such work in PSE and assemblies. Two state that relationships are 'not mentioned much in assemblies', though one says they are 'often discussed in tutorials and this is helped by the group getting on with and being able to talk to the tutor'. A Year 11 girl thinks pupils generally get on well together but that when they do not intervention makes little difference or even 'can make situations worse and if you tell a teacher then this can lead to a fight with the pupil involved'. A girl in Year 8 reiterates this risk of 'recriminations' but acknowledges that disclosure is important: 'Sometimes talking to a teacher can get you in more trouble with pupils but it is generally important and useful to sort out problems.' She adds that different pupils want different levels of teacher intervention and that 'some don't want teachers knowing pupils' business'. One of the pupils wrote on the questionnaire: 'I think kids would get along better without the teachers butting in, because they make matters worse.'

This mixed feeling among pupils on the extent of teacher helpfulness is reflected in the variety of comments on fights. One pupil wrote: 'When people get into fights we all stand around as if it is a sport. There is a fight every month.' Another wrote that only eight or ten times do arguments lead to a fight and that teachers could stop it if 'they did a little more about their punishment'. Fighting is mentioned as being successfully interrupted by five of the pupils interviewed. A Year 7 boy says: 'Teachers do see and stop most fights and few go unnoticed.' This seems to be the consensus and most, like a Year 8 boy, feel that it is followed up satisfactorily: 'If a fight takes place, after it is broken up the staff will try to find out what it was about.' A Year 11 boy who retaliated physically to a physical attack and did not like it 'once it became physical', is pleased that 'the teachers took an interest and kept an eye on the other pupil'. The same boy praises the teachers who involved the police to deal with a large fight off school property involving some of the school's pupils and people from outside school. The deputy headteacher's statement that 'most cases in Years 7, 8 and 9 are dealt with effectively', is confirmed strongly by four of the pupils interviewed. The Year 7 boy reflects the majority feeling that there is a general approach made by teachers

> to split up people involved and give a detention to them. All pupils are treated the same and teachers are fair. They all seem to be able to deal with incidents. Teachers always make things better.

The pupils' interviews also exemplify to some extent an awareness of procedures as outlined here by the head of Year 9.

> The report strategy and follow up with bullies encourages discussion and review of the evidence in the report. In the main school deals with its own problems. Three cases last year went to head and governors. They were suspended, one permanently. Most cases are dealt with by year heads and pastoral team. Extreme cases are often of psychological nature and need special needs care.

Pupils interviewed show awareness of some kind of reporting procedure, the clearest being a Year 11 boy who explained it as 'a policy illustrated in the Code of Behaviour, report system, and stage system of actions taken. We are told about this in school'. A written comment was: 'If I did have any problems then I would go to my form tutor and she would take it seriously and talk to me about it in confidence.'

The head of Year 9 involves parents in the first stage of the process and, although 'it is very time consuming', he believes that 'if we can work with parents there is more chance of success'. The deputy head affirms that 'contact with parents is good and that bullying is mentioned more by parents than pupils'. Nearly all the pupils interviewed share this view that parents are important both in school and at home in helping to sort out problems. One girl thinks: 'Parents can sort it out. For example they talk to teachers who listen to them more if they are angry.' One boy believes that 'family is important as pupils will be talked to and told off and realize they can't get away with bad behaviour'. However, one pupil wrote: 'I don't tell my mum about fights in school or she will worry about me.'

## Problems

The school's anti-bullying policy relies entirely on those involved knowing and understanding it as implicit in a general behaviour code and not as one written specifically as anti-bullying. Evidence suggests this may lead to inconsistent practice and victims of bullying slipping through the net. Interviews show that most pupils think teachers are inconsistent when dealing with bullying situations. One girl in Year 8 says: 'Sometimes teachers deal with trouble very well by following up an event but others don't and this is bad.' Another feels there is discrimination and that if 'teachers split up a fight they take the pupils concerned to the head but if it is a prefect it's more likely they will just be reported'. One girl doubts the effectiveness of the reporting system: 'Even though you get put on report or suspended if your behaviour is bad, some pupils don't change even after that. Some pupils don't react to intervention by teachers if they are egged on by other pupils.'

Pupils' writings indicate a strong awareness of bullying with some acceptance of it with comments like: 'People don't get bullied too often, it's just now and again'; 'Sometimes people have a go at me but it's usually a joke and not serious at all'; and 'Bullying is part of school life and growing up.' Non-accepting attitudes are shown too with: 'It should be controlled like our school does'; and 'Some people can be very horrible to others and will not leave them alone. I hope something can be done about this.' There were written references to sexual harassment like average-size girls being picked on for being fat by 'skinny' boys, and 'if someone touches you "privately" it usually gets laughed off. I don't think schools are safe places, not if this is allowed to happen . . . it's disgusting.' Another wrote that: 'Bullies work in groups. If they are with friends they would bully you but if they are alone they want you to hang around with them.'

These written comments, combined with the survey evidence of 12 per cent of pupils having been physically bullied often, suggest that some incidents are not being dealt with by the policy. This may be in part due to bullying issues being just one element in an overall behaviour policy rather than being prioritized or specifically focused on. Several comments from staff suggest this may be the case. A head of year refers to 'regular meetings to discuss pupils' progress and bullying is usually low on the agenda'. A tutor likewise feels that:

> Bullying as an issue does not come up that often. It is not a high priority and there are usually other issues such as uniforms, homework, attitude and motivation. In Year 8 only three bullying incidents were dealt with there and then with no later recurrence.

The school's successful pastoral programme enables and encourages discussions of bullying in terms of relationships and the senior teacher thinks: 'This policy is least problematic when the issues are raised in PSE and other programmes.' However, she believes that 'most problems arise in instances or cases that have to be actually dealt with'. For her, the major problem is identifying bullies and bullied. The deputy headteacher also acknowledges that:

> bullying goes on – name-calling, verbal and other non physical violence like 'funny looks' being a threat. We try to nip it in the bud. Our

problem lies in identifying it, or pupils/parents reporting it. Specific evidence of incidents is hard to come by. Sometimes pupils bring them to our attention and we deal with them.

One of the tutors reiterates this difficulty:

A big problem is 'trivial' name-calling. Verbal rather than physical abuse is a problem. It is easily dealt with, however, when it arises but it is difficult to detect. Girls do verbal bullying and are covert about it. Boys tend to be more direct and physical and therefore more noticeable. The head of Year 9 has difficulty getting evidence and getting pupils to come forward.

A written, publicized policy specifically on anti-bullying may alert more pupils to the structures and procedures which are already in existence. Most of the pupils interviewed are aware of a policy although not all are totally clear what it is. This uncertainty may deter pupils taking the risk of disclosing bearing in mind the known inconsistencies of responses by teachers and the risk of recriminations. As one teacher put it:

The bullied and bullies need to know there is a system they can turn to. Many of the pupils experience problems at home and need justice and support at school. Pupil social deprivation is closely linked with bullying and we know that bullies have often been bullied at home. The main problem for one of the tutors 'is getting to the bottom of things' and what was the cause but we stick to it and investigate until we get to the truth. Pupils know this.

However, this may not be the case for all pupils and as another tutor points out the situations change from year to year.

Bullying can sometimes run in a 'bad year' rather than consistently across years. Often it is not one-to-one bullying but four or five boys acting anti-socially to everyone: staff and pupils alike.

The extent to which pupils help each other in solving bullying problems is mentioned more specifically by the pupils than teachers. Only two of the pupils interviewed think that friends are helpful. One feels that they are only important if the people involved actually want them to play a part. Another says he is unlikely to listen to friends as he does not feel he has to and another boy thinks friends are not listened to by the parties in a dispute as they are not seen as having any authority. One girl believes friends could even stir up more trouble.

Problems arise if values are not shared and known by all members of the community for various reasons such as when new people come to the school and have not grown up with the generally known system. One tutor says: 'If we've had pupils over the five years we are more likely to be successful. However, some of our "imports" remain problems because they have not grown up with our routine and regulations.' Other problems arise sometimes if events take place and not everyone involved is fully informed, such as the form tutor who sometimes feels: 'I am the last to know about an exclusion.'

The subtleties of the bullying behaviours and issues may mean that it needs to be dealt with on several levels and that perhaps an unwritten policy on anti-bullying, although it works well, may benefit further from being formalized in writing to promote more awareness and clarity. According to a Year 9 tutor:

> The problem with bullying is that it is diverse. Obvious signs are easy to deal with. It's the more subtle types that are difficult. We need to use hard evidence when dealing with bullies because they are not aware of being bullies themselves.

The crucial work of discussions and awareness raising is taking place through the pastoral system and the pupil and teacher interviews show that pupils generally feel safe and happy in school. This is an enormous achievement bearing in mind the deprivation of the catchment area. However, the figures in the survey show a high level of physical bullying and this suggests that the process is still in the early stages.

---

**Reflection**   One of the underlying problems where there is no policy is that matters of communication may be overlooked. What advantages and disadvantages do you consider exist for effective communications at Oakley?

---

### The way forward

There are several plans for further reducing bullying and staff see the next steps in terms of building on and extending an already successful system. The main ideas are:

- finding more ways to encourage disclosures;
- integrating the behaviour code more fully into the curriculum with full staff support;
- using monitoring to get more information;
- rewards for good pupil behaviour; and
- building primary liaison and links with outside agencies.

The senior teacher envisages the senior management team having a strong role to 'reinforce support for all this'. One of the tutors feels that something else needs to be done about the fact that there are more problems than we see. We need to look beyond the cases that come to our attention. In the main staff are approachable and we are a small school. Most cases are reported by pupils or parents but what about cases that are not reported. Perhaps we could have a box to alert us anonymously.

The pupils' ideas on the ideal forms of intervention centre around respect for each other and the teachers with comments like 'everyone should be treated as an individual' and 'only do things to people that you would like done to you' which applies to teachers as well as pupils. They draw attention to specific problems such as 'sometimes you get a gang together and they look down on anyone who doesn't dress like them or does the same things as them'. Also they mentioned specific strategies for teachers such as 'listening to pupils and giving them a chance to say what they think', 'listen to everyone's side of the story', 'pupils having someone in the school to talk to – an adult' and 'certain teachers should form a sort of council at dinner times, and pupils who are concerned should go and talk to them'. One suggests that 'teachers should keep a look out down corridors' and 'should keep their eyes open at all times to help cut the amount of fighting', and a practical idea is for 'more facilities for pupils at breaks and lunch-times to give pupils more to do and they would therefore be less likely to argue out of boredom'. Concern was shown about 'bullies sometimes having problems of their own and they only bully to try and get rid of their problems. If they were maybe talked to by someone, things could get sorted out for them.' Another idea is for 'occasional year assemblies about bullying, and if bullies are sitting there it may make them think twice about what they are doing'.

## Downlands High School

This school has a similar catchment to Oakley High School in terms of social class but is twice the size with about 1000 pupils aged 11–16 years, 56 teachers and an average class size of 23 pupils. It serves a large council housing estate in a city suburb with a high proportion of disadvantaged people and above-average unemployment. The pupils cover the whole ability range biased towards lower abilities. About 7 per cent of pupils are from ethnic minorities and 28 per cent of pupils are eligible for free meals. Probably due to its size, location and some accommodation difficulties (which according to the 1994 Ofsted report 'reduces their opportunities to act responsibly'), there is a somewhat boisterous atmosphere. The survey shows higher than average reports of verbal and physical bullying and property abuse. Nine per cent reported being physically bullied often. Ofsted describes the school as an orderly community but expresses some concerns about a lack of consistency in responses to mis-behaviour even though the behaviour policy contains sound procedures for the prevention and dealing with it. It acknowledges good practice such as celebrating positive work and behaviour and the recently adopted anti-bullying policy which it says should be monitored and implemented consistently and effectively. It refers to the school seeking 'to combat all forms of bullying through the curriculum and through the whole-school ethos'. Interviews suggests that much effort and some progress has been made since Ofsted to continue promoting a safe, caring environment. However, many staff comment on progress being impeded by external influences which are often at variance with the school's. The school is further along in the continuum of change because it has been operating specific strategies from a formal written anti-bullying policy for four years, has reflected on progress made and has initiated the next phase towards pupils' self-help. A total of 112 pupils were surveyed, with five written comments (4.3 per cent of the cohort) and five pupils and five teachers were interviewed.

### Establishing policy

A whole-school working party including governors was set up in 1993 in response to an increase in bullying incidents. After six months of seeking advice from outside bodies and other schools, it presented a draft to a full staff meeting but with no formal in-service training. This written policy is currently being reviewed with pupils having an input via a newly formed youth action group. It consists of: a statement of its aims; a definition of bullying and a list of its manifestations; a statement of intent; strategies for prevention and management of incidents and handouts giving clear guid-ance to visitors, pupils, support staff, site supervisors and janitors, lunch-time supervisors, teaching staff and parents. The aims are:

- to create a climate in school whereby bullying behaviour is not accepted by any member of the school community including parents;
- to implement strategies for all pupils, staff and parents to work toward the elimination of bullying;
- to establish effective procedures to identify and deal with bullying if and when it occurs;
- to make use of the curriculum to raise awareness of what bullying is and the school's expectations;
- to provide ongoing support and counselling for both victims and bul-lies;
- to involve outside professional agencies if and where necessary and helpful.

The schools definition of bullying and statement of intent is made clear in the following document.

**Downlands High School**

BULLYING TAKES PLACE IN ALL SCHOOLS.
BULLYING IS THE WILFUL, CONSCIOUS DESIRE TO HURT OR
    THREATEN OR FRIGHTEN SOMEONE ELSE.
BULLYING CAN TAKE MANY DIFFERENT FORMS.
BULLYING CAN BE:
  Damage to property
  Graffiti
  Borrowing without permission
  Vandalism
  Silent pressure
  Ignoring
  Refusing to sit next to
  Group pressure
  Invading privacy
  Name-calling
  Ridicule
  Spreading rumours
  Passing notes
  Heckling
  Fighting
  Extortion
  Intimidation
  Physical violence
  Incitement

<u>BULLYING WILL NOT BE TOLERATED AT DOWNLANDS HIGH
SCHOOL</u>

At Downlands High School we want our school to be a welcoming
place where children are happy and relaxed enough to take full
advantage of all the educational opportunities we have to offer. We
seek to create a climate in school where bullying behaviour is not
accepted by any member of the school community.
In order to achieve this we must have a clear commitment to
oppose all forms of bullying. We must have effective procedures in
place to deal with bullying and these must be effective in dealing
with both perpetrator and victim. The procedures will include a
Bullying Incident Report Sheet and opportunities for counselling
both bully and victim.
The Downlands High School Policy applies to the whole school
community, including pupils, parents, and staff and emanates from
a working group that reflects a cross-section of this community.

The policy takes account of a school curriculum that allows pupils to learn how to interact with others and encourages them to talk about bullying. By means of applying its anti-bullying policy the school seeks to create an environment where the opportunities to bully are limited.

The school's statement and policy to oppose bullying is consistent with the principles that underpin our anti-racist policy and is firmly based on our equal opportunities philosophy. This policy will be regularly reviewed within the framework of a democratic school structure that lays down positive values on how we think we should relate to each other.

In order to be successful in achieving our anti-bullying policy it is recognized that resources will need to be made available where possible in terms of finance, INSET, curriculum support materials and improving staffing levels.

Downlands High School is opposed to all forms of bullying. Collectively, our policy and guidelines offer the means to deal with the bully and offer support to the victim. It is our aim to eradicate all forms of bullying from our school community.

1  If any of the above takes place in the classroom, then the teacher should be informed at once in a calm manner.
2  If any of the above takes place on the yard/corridors/toilets etc. then this should be reported to a member of staff at once.
3  If at any time there is no one to report to, then the next step would be to contact your form teacher, or your head of year or a senior member of staff.
4  If you cannot tell any of these people, tell your parents and ask them to contact the school.

Any report will be recorded and fully investigated.

IF YOU ARE UNHAPPY WITH WHAT HAS BEEN DONE, THEN CONTACT ONE OF THE DEPUTIES OR THE HEADTEACHER

Pupils are given guidelines which list the types of bullying behaviour and the instructions (see 1–4 in box) on what to do if they experience any of them. Lunch-time supervisors, administrative staff, caretakers and cleaning staff work in places where bullying occurs and the importance of their role is reflected in their own specific guidelines. Teachers are given guidelines on the implementation of anti-bullying policy.

**Downlands High School**

GUIDELINES ON THE IMPLEMENTATION OF OUR ANTI-
BULLYING POLICY: TEACHING STAFF

BULLYING IS THE WILFUL, CONSCIOUS DESIRE TO HURT OR
THREATEN OR FRIGHTEN SOMEONE ELSE

1 Deal with the incident.
2 Identify the pupils involved in the incident.
3 Fill in the Bullying Incident Sheet from the file located in the
  staffroom.
4 Fill in the Form Teacher Information Slip(s) from the folder
  located in the staffroom and place in the appropriate staff pigeon
  hole(s).
AT THIS POINT THE REFERRAL PROCEDURE IS DETERMINED
BY THE SERIOUSNESS OF THE INCIDENT

When dealing with a bullying incident the following procedures
will prove helpful:
1 Ask the victim to record the events in writing.
2 Ask the bully to record the events in writing.
3 Staff (at whichever level of seniority) should record the
  discussion with both parties.
4 Letters should be written to the parents of both bully and victim
  outlining the nature of the incident.
5 Discuss the bullying incident with the parents – by telephone or
  by appointment in school.
6 Make the point to the bully by removal of privileges.
7 In severe cases, exclusion from school may be appropriate.

A handout for parents ('What Action May Be Taken?') (see p. 130) gives them advice and lists the types of behaviour which are regarded by the school as bullying.

### Policy into practice

The written policy aimed at all personnel covers all eventualities and strongly attempts to influence parents towards its ethical stance on bullying. Staff and pupil interviews suggest that many parents are not convinced and hold a very different view. Within school, the way the policy is perceived and practised is also varied and the headteacher finds that shared values are difficult to maintain when even a small minority of staff

**Downlands High School**

WHAT ACTION MAY BE TAKEN?

ALL reported incidents of bullying will be recorded and action will
be taken. This will involve the use of sanctions. If the headteacher
becomes aware of persistent or serious offences, then parents,
governors, or the police may be involved. Serious offences could
result in the permanent exclusion of the offender from Downlands
High School.

WHAT SHOULD YOU DO IF YOUR CHILD IS THE VICTIM OF
BULLYING BEHAVIOUR?

(a)  If it happens in school?
Ensure that the school has been informed. If you find that your
child has not told anyone at school, please contact the school office.
Your complaint will be treated seriously, thoroughly investigated,
the appropriate action will be taken within school and you will be
advised of the outcome. In the more serious cases you could be
advised in addition to contact the appropriate outside agency.
IF YOU FEEL UNHAPPY ABOUT THE WAY THE INCIDENT
HAS BEEN DEALT WITH, YOU ARE STRONGLY
RECOMMENDED TO CONTACT THE HEADTEACHER.

(b)  If it happens outside school?
 In such an event we would advise that if the offence is serious or
there is persistent harassment, you should inform the police or
seek further advice from the appropriate agencies.
It would be helpful if you could inform the headteacher so that we
can monitor the situation in school.

WHAT SHOULD YOU DO IF YOUR CHILD IS INVOLVED IN
BULLYING BEHAVIOUR?
It is far more effective if the children can see we are all working
together. You can therefore, help by supporting the action taken by
the school and explaining it to your child that bullying behaviour is
TOTALLY UNACCEPTABLE. If pupils see that parents and school
are united in this matter it will help discourage such behaviour.

'do not accept or understand them'. Those interviewed appear to see the
policy more as a means to deal with incidents than as a guide on how to
prevent them with 'a line of how an issue goes up the hierarchical system,
i.e. who reports to whom'.

Four of the pupils interviewed are happy at school and generally satisfied with the friendly atmosphere. Most say they experience the policy through learning about relationships in form periods 'where we are warned about behaviour and told what is expected, and in PSE but with no examples given'. Teachers hold the same view that the policy is to be delivered through PSE and assemblies where children were to be made aware of styles of bullying and there is no mention of work across the rest of the curriculum. According to one tutor:

There is an awareness of the policy and the aim is to build up relationships and foster understanding in pastoral groups but staff will put their subjects' priorities first. This is the same with staff development – there are courses but staff put their subjects first.

Part of the policy is a document on strategies which includes ideas for using the school curriculum as 'a vehicle for activities designed to prevent the incidence of bullying' yet interviews suggest the focus is solely in the pastoral curriculum rather than in National Curriculum subject areas. The strategies document advocates appropriate teaching methods such as 'good use of praise/reprimand in dealing with appropriate behaviour' and 'teaching and learning styles, e.g. group work and cooperative practices'. It also refers to the 'hidden curriculum' and 'good role models, school ethos, supervision issues, policy and practice regarding anti-racism, gender, pupils with special educational needs and disability'. Staff do not mention any of these strategies specifically and a few say there is no link between an awareness of bullying and the curriculum.

## Monitoring

The number and nature of incidents are regarded as performance indicators. Although no specific figures are given, staff interviewed say more pupils are disclosing incidents and have a greater willingness to talk and share problems than before. This is felt to be across the age range with a predominance in the younger pupils. No mention of other surveys on bullying are mentioned apart from this project's questionnaire and one planned by the youth action group.

## Successes

Teachers are clearly aware of the procedures to take regarding bullying incidents with classroom teachers being the first point of contact and knowing whom to inform next. Pupils seem more vague about this although they noticed particular strategies used by their teachers and know that they are supposed to refer problems to the heads of year and 'let them sort it out'. Teacher intervention is seen as usually successful though as one boy puts it 'they sometimes make the problem worse'. This boy, who was physically hurt after having a brick thrown at his head, says he was not worried by it. He told the year head who dealt directly with the bully giving her detention and lines. This satisfied him but he wants more measures to prevent incidents before they happen. The most effective and speedy types of intervention referred to by pupils are separating those in conflict 'so they could think while apart and often become friends again', splitting up fights and sending pupils out of classrooms. A type of preventative work noticed by one of the pupils was separating primary school pupils on entry to the school in Year 7 to encourage new friendships. Staff interviews reveal a high priority given to promoting happy and secure relationships and all pupils interviewed refer to relationships and friendships as one of the most enjoyable aspects of school. One girl sums this with 'we have to get along and be friendly otherwise there would be war'. For another girl her friends are 'the only good thing' and help her to 'get through' school.

Counselling recipients of bullying is viewed as an effective way to enable them to take charge of the situations themselves so that bullying stops. So far this has been done by teachers and a training course for pupils to be peer counsellors has also been initiated. Enabling pupils to act assertively for themselves is seen as preferable to someone else giving them advice or stopping the bullying. Various counselling strategies were constructed from the policy's strategies document.

---

**Downlands High School**

COUNSELLING STRATEGIES

Whoever the counsellor, the following steps may provide a useful framework for support:

| | |
|---|---|
| *listen* | try to understand the full implications of the problem for the person |
| *focus* | help the person become more specific about the problem |
| *prioritize* | find the most important aspect of the problem |
| *brainstorm* | consider lots of possible ways of dealing with the problem |
| *plan* | decide on the best course of action – consider what may go wrong |
| *action* | the plan into action |
| *support* | consider whether support is required to implement the plan |
| *evaluate* | decide whether any changes need to be made |

---

Although there are clearly many achievements with the policy more pupils than teachers refer to them in terms of 'success'. For example, two pupils interviewed mention the success of bringing parents into school. The teachers, however, when asked about successes, only refer to INSET being available and opportunities for newly qualified teachers. The head-teacher, outlines a major recent success with the participation of two senior teachers, two heads of year, a classroom teacher and a learning support teacher on a co-counselling course funded by an international bank. They have recently finished the course to increase support for themselves and their colleagues as well as planning to support Year 10 pupils to set up a peer counselling service which is mentioned later. Their enthusiasm for the course has encouraged more teachers to enrol on a similar one next year.

## Problems

The teachers seem more aware of the policy's existence than the pupils. Of the latter, neither those interviewed nor those who wrote comments referred to an anti-bullying policy as such and one boy interviewed said he knew of no policies about pupil–pupil behaviour. The only policy men-tioned in the interviews was the Code of Conduct and the girl who referred to it felt it was mostly ignored. She was unhappy at school and believed that pupil–pupil and pupil–staff relationships needed to be improved. Teachers, she felt, were in many cases not aware of what was happening so could not intervene and when they did it 'only worked with minor problems but not major ones'. She was especially concerned about 'major racism problems' and advocated 'raising awareness and more def-inite punishments for offenders'. Four of the written comments echoed this with a call for 'harder punishments'. One of the pupils wrote they were 'needed or people will get away too easily'. Another wrote: 'People who behave badly again and again seem to get told off less than those who just misbehave once. I think this should be the other way around.'

Although more pupils are disclosing bullying incidents, some staff are of the opinion that the policy has been 'less effective than the school would have wished. The environment in which the children live conflicts with anti-bullying ideas.' The pupils interviewed indicate a feeling that teachers do their best to stop bullying and are in most cases successful but with some serious exceptions which are often due to a lack of awareness or ineffective handling. The written comments are all concerned with these exceptions. One pupil wrote: 'Schools and headmasters are soft. Even teachers ignore bullying and just walk past without saying any-thing.' Another pupil wrote of taking the law into his own hands when he is bullied: 'On the way home you should not get told off for fighting. People call me "Big Chin" but I am not bothered. I tell them to get off. I punch people if they annoy me.'

The last quotation highlights a mismatch of school and community values which is a constant theme in both sets of interview data and pupils' written comments. The headteacher gives the following example: 'I interviewed the parents of a boy whom we suspended for bullying and the father agreed that the boy should be punished but only because he was found out.' He also refers to a mother of two new pupils from Years 7 and 8 who told him that their father, from whom she was separated because of his violence, had in the past bribed children to bully his own children in order to avenge himself on her: 'She wanted me to ensure if there was any bullying of her children that it was "genuine" bullying and not incited by their father.' Two pupils interviewed echo this type of situation by referring to 'a variety of family roles not always having a good effect' on pupils. One comments on parents being often involved but then having 'various attitudes' towards incidents 'sometimes resulting in them not helping'. Another pupil likewise sees problems in involving parents who 'usually make it worse for the person who is in trouble'. However, another believes it would help to involve parents earlier especially in punishments.

The most common concern of the headteacher and his staff is the hostile environment in which they were trying to promote anti-bullying values. This is vividly exemplified by the headteacher's comment on trouble caused by or involving young people from outside the school and his specific referral to 'a gang of Asian boys from outside our catchment area who attacked some white Year 7 pupils in retaliation for attacks on them by pupils in our school'.

### The way forward

The next step seems to be in encouraging the pupils to play a bigger role in the policy. One of the teachers hopes that the youth action group will continue to meet. The ideal intervention for one of the girls interviewed was for good relationships between pupils to be verbally encouraged by staff. There is a shift of focus to self-help in the form of peer and co-counselling involving pupils from Year 10 and a cross-section of staff as referred to above. In September 1997 the school embarked alongside Greendale High School and a special school in a two-year project funded by the international bank mentioned earlier. The intention is to set up a peer counselling service whereby pupils help and empower each other. It also involves meeting pupils from the other schools to set up co-counselling relationships with them, the idea being to break down the barriers of social class and perceived ability levels.

> **Reflection**   Given the range of pressures upon schools and the passing of groups through the system, how can interest in topics such as behaviour management be maintained by staff and pupils?

## Greendale High School

With about 1240 pupils this school is much larger than the previous two schools and provides the project with the biggest percentage of the sample. It is an 11–18 mixed comprehensive school situated on a large, mostly owner-occupied, housing estate on the edge of a medium-size town. It is popular and oversubscribed, serving a suburb of another small town as well as the immediate neighbourhood. The majority of pupils are socially advantaged with numbers eligible for school meals low at 2.5 per cent. There are 67.5 teaching staff and the average teaching group size is 25 pupils in overcrowded accommodation. The attainment of pupils covers the whole range but is generally high. The Ofsted report in March 1996 is very favourable referring to the school as 'a well ordered community. Behaviour is very good in and around school, reflecting the high expectations of staff and pupils'. It also says: 'The school creates a supportive environment in which pupils feel safe, happy and well cared for. Bullying is dealt with speedily and successfully.' It is furthest along the continuum of change having actively pursued and monitored a policy for six years. Two surveys were completed in 1993 and 1995 to ascertain pupil attitudes to bullying and a variety of strategies have raised discussion and awareness of the issue. The numbers of parents' complaints have reduced, and there are fewer serious incidents reported although the Keele survey shows that frequent verbal bullying is higher than the norm, 4 per cent being physically bullied often is one of the eight lowest percentages in the sample and figures suggest it has the seventh lowest percentage of bullies; 242 pupils were surveyed with 37 written responses (14.9 per cent of the cohort) and four pupils and five teachers were interviewed.

### Establishing policy

The headteacher describes the policy as evolving from an ethos of 'caring and support which is deep rooted and firmly established'. The senior teacher emphasizes the importance of relationships to effective learning and how 'it is in the school's best interest to maintain the very healthy relationships which are formed from a strong pastoral care system'. In 1990 pupils from the school council and the school counsellor perceived bullying as a whole-school relationships problem which needed to be addressed by the whole community rather than by individuals and initiated a proactive approach. The police and a national campaigning charity funded and publicized a whole-school day workshop with pupil and staff representatives from other town schools. It was led by the school counsellor and Michele Elliot, director of Kidscape. In follow-up discussions involving all pupils the consensus was to have a whole-school anti-bullying policy, a contract signed by all pupils and a peer counselling service run by pupils. This unwritten policy initiated in 1991 was coordinated by an anti-bullying working party, including pupils, which oversaw the peer counselling scheme, the anti-bullying contracts, theatre productions and a survey. The senior teacher describes the policy as 'natural and relevant' and its development as 'piecemeal within the progressive development of

---

**Greendale High School**

This policy reflects the school's commitment to equal opportunities.
The school defines bullying as follows:

Bullying is unacceptable behaviour which results in somebody feeling hurt, threatened or frightened. This can be physical or verbal and includes hitting, teasing, intimidation, ostracizing, damaging a person's property as well as racial, sexual and disability harassment.

- All pupils sign an anti-bullying contract.
- The definition and guidelines for pupil behaviour are posted on boards throughout the school.
- There is a clear procedure to follow should bullying occur and everyone knows what it is.
- There is a support system for victims and survivors of bullying including the school counsellor and a peer counselling service called the Pupil Helper Scheme.
- Pupil Helpers are trained to teach basic listening and counselling skills to the lower school.
- There is a sanctions and support system for bullies, including counselling as above.
- Non-aggressive behaviour is recognized through the rewards system.
- The school's physical environment and general organization is designed to minimize bullying behaviour.
- There is the opportunity for full involvement of teaching and non-teaching staff, governors, parents and pupils in discussion and implementation of the anti-bullying policy.
- The curriculum includes:
  (1) A PSE programme for pupils to discuss, support, monitor and update the policy.
  (2) Assemblies, drama productions, certain teaching programmes and other means of raising awareness on the subject.

the school's PSE programme'. In 1995, the policy (on page 136) was formalized by the working party into a short written document to give the school's definition of bullying, to state current practice and to clarify future intentions. It is reproduced in the staff handbook and posted in classrooms and corridors along with procedures to be taken if bullied.

## Policy into practice

All staff interviews reveal a common understanding of the principles underlying the policy with comments like: 'the respect and rights of the individual'; 'opportunities for a secure school life for all across the age and ability range'; and 'providing a caring community'. The headteacher believes the principle underlying the policy is 'a climate of expecting respect of each other so that all members of the school community are able to talk openly about issues'. He emphasizes the importance of pupils being able to 'divulge and share'. The Ofsted report likewise draws attention to how pupils 'effectively support each other, both informally and through the counselling service, which is valued highly by pupils and parents'.

The anti-bullying process has a high pupil participation and leadership, especially in the peer and co-counselling service and this relies on a small number of staff across the hierarchy playing a major role as allies. As the headteacher points out, the process was influenced in the main by two key members of staff, the pastoral deputy head and the school counsellor who 'wanted to see the school develop in a new way'. In addition, 'the overall influence in recent years has been the part played by staff below senior management level'. A senior teacher and the head of Year 7 both emphasized that the policy did not arise from a crisis as 'bullying has never been a major issue in the school' but it was 'something we ought to have so that the whole school community are aware'. It was seen as an aspect of the whole-school equal opportunities policy also being developed, established and accepted in parallel. The Year 7 head explains that the anti-bullying policy is founded on the principle of a sharing approach 'which has been established through a counselling system based on approachability'. The peer counsellors are trained to listen and support recipients and perpetrators of bullying wanting confidential help. To be fully effective they work on their own self-development by co-counselling with each other in pairs and in support groups. One of the tutors explained that in this way they can use their skills productively when there are 'no customers'. Co-counselling has been in operation since 1984 when the school counsellor began teaching courses to about 40 volunteers a year from Years 11, 12 and 13. The pupils learned the Re-evaluation Counselling model and some followed it up with further courses outside school. Since 1992 she has trained about 50 volunteers a year from Years 11, 12 and 13, 40 of whom became active peer counsellors as well as counselling each other. They visit Years 7 and 8 tutor groups once a week during tutor periods to teach listening and co-counselling skills and lead quality circles and self-esteem games. Pupils are told they can have private listening time for problems at other times, either with a teacher or a pupil peer counsellor. The service which includes a lunch-time 'drop in' is publicized in assemblies and posters with an emphasis on the service's confidentiality, except in extreme cases. Peer counsellors' skills are acknowledged in their Records of Achievement and they are supervised and supported weekly by the school counsellor during lunch-breaks and morning registration times. In these meetings they plan activities with tutor groups, celebrate successes and discuss problems, using co-counselling as a tool for helping each other. At first there were more peer counsellors than there were 'clients' but with more publicity it became part of everyday school life with increasing numbers of pupils being counselled by them on bullying and a variety of other problems. An extract from one of Greendale's 1993 documents shows how peer counselling was considered central to the development of an anti-bullying policy.

---

### Greendale High School

PEER COUNSELLING

Greendale High is beginning to bring the whole issue of bullying into the open so that the focus is away from individuals. As a result it is hoped that the climate in the school is becoming safer and friendlier. In the past when pupils were bullied many of them saw the situation as a shameful individual problem, often blaming themselves and suffering in silence for fear of reprisals. This attitude is changing so that survivors of bullying take action to stop it re-occurring and bullies come to realize that they themselves have a problem which is causing their bullying behaviour. Both bullies and survivors are offered counselling and many take it up. Many volunteer to become pupil helpers themselves.

What is valuable about the policy is the on-going process of it as much as the end results. It involves and empowers the pupils. The anti-bullying policy is talked about openly and regularly so that everyone is clear about what the whole school considers bullying behaviour to be and that it is not acceptable. Bullying still happens but at least it is not so much underground and more survivors are coming forward to get it stopped. When they ask for help action is taken to stop it. Bullies also come forward and ask for help and are given it. Many young people are learning how to co-counsel and this enables them to deal with many other problems they have in school.

Another aspect of the anti-bullying policy is the contract initiated in 1992 when the pupils voted on which format and words to adopt from those they had suggested at the end of the day workshop in 1991. The contract (reproduced in Chapter 5; see page 65) has since been signed by all pupils and their parents on joining the school. The headteacher says it is one of only a few contracts so that its importance is emphasized. Pupils who wrote comments approved of it with statements like 'I think our school is good because we have an anti-bullying form which every pupil has to sign, whether they sign to stick to it or not' and 'Anti-bullying forms should be used in all schools everywhere in USA, England, etc.' The contract is introduced at the beginning of Year 7 by a worksheet in the pupils' PSE booklet.

---

**Greendale High School**

CONTRACT

BULLYING

In any large working environment it is important that people can live and work together. Imagine the problems that could occur if people argued constantly and were unable to feel comfortable. Schools and places of work can work efficiently when people display patience and understanding.

WRITTEN WORK
What is bullying?
1  Privately make a note in your textbook of any type of action that you think may be considered as bullying and explain the reasons why.
2  When you have completed your list compare your answers with a friend and see if the reasons why you thought an action was bullying are the same.
3  Class discussion of answers.
4  Think about a time when you may have been bullied yourself or about a time when you may have seen someone else being bullied.
   (a) Write a paragraph explaining the incident.
   (b) Explain how you think the person being bullied felt.
   (c) What do you think were the reasons behind the bully's action?

At Greendale it is important that everybody works together to prevent bullying from taking place. In order to minimize bullying at school every pupil and parent are given an anti-bullying contract to read and sign. This is an agreement that was devised by pupils themselves in order to promote good relationships in school with all pupils. The following three points are what each child agrees to. Read each statement and in your textbook explain what each point means.

(a) I will treat all my fellow pupils with respect.

(b) I will not humiliate or hurt any other pupil physically or verbally.

(c) I will do the best I can to help any pupil who is obviously being upset or hurt by one or more other pupils.

Anti-bullying work is covered in all year groups' PSE work and the peer counsellors work across all age groups. It also takes place in other areas of the curriculum and all staff indicate an awareness that the issues relate to subject areas. A newly qualified teacher realizes that 'bullying is not just a playground thing' and work in English, history, drama and dance is specifically mentioned by others. The head of Year 7 thinks 'a good class teacher differentiates work to avoid a sense of failure when working on this topic'. The headteacher feels that the school has 'the advantage of

**ME**

I used to think it great fun
Watching them pick on her
Being so bitchy
It must have really hurt
It used to be quite funny
Until I looked to see
That it wasn't her they were picking on
But this time it was me

I wished I hadn't laughed now
Because it aches inside
The trouble that they cause me
Was far too much to hide
Now I know what it feels like
Being picked on time after time
I now know not to laugh at them
And that bullying is a crime

Kathryn Bellamy

organizing and administering a homogeneous group so it is easier to operate a total approach which is less fragmented as a result of fewer pressures.
We can seem to be consistent as a result.' The school sent in documentary
evidence of work programmes and pupils' work where the issues are
'exposed and explored'. A poem written in an English lesson by a Year 10
girl, later published in a national newspaper and a poetry anthology, is
reproduced on page 140.

## Monitoring

The three main methods used by the school to formally monitor bullying
are: surveys; incidences recorded and collated by heads of year and the
coordinator of equal opportunities; and pupils' self-reports in a problem
box. The counsellor also keeps a record of the number of pupils who go
to her or peer counsellors because of bullying. Before the Keele Partnership survey there were two others conducted jointly with the County
Health Promotion Unit with a 100 per cent survey of Years 7 and 8. In 1993
attitudes were surveyed and in 1995 they measured changes in attitude
since 1993 and the nature and extent of bullying and friendly behaviour
experienced in one week. The data showed improved attitudes with less
tolerance of bullying and the working party intends to compare the
nature and extent of bullying with that for all schools in the Keele Partnership survey.

## Successes

The Ofsted report acknowledges the anti-bullying work in the following
way:

> The extensive programme of work against bullying is effective.
> Pupils feel secure in the established procedures should bullying
> occur. Parents share the view that when incidents of bullying occur,
> they are dealt with promptly and effectively . . . [Pupils] co-operate
> with each other and are mutually supportive [and] feel they can turn
> to staff at a variety of levels for support and are happy and secure in
> school.

This view is confirmed by the pupil interviews where they all refer to
friendships with peers and friendly teachers being two good aspects about
school. They use words like 'supportive', 'caring', 'loyalty' and 'depend-
ability' when describing the importance of relationships to them. Most of
the written comments regarding the ethos of the school supported this
view and the following comment is typical:

Greendale High is a lovely school to be in. People are friendly, but sometimes there is an outburst but in my case nothing ever really lasts long and I am hardly ever hurt or abused. My parents love me, trust me and understand me. I love school and can't wait for the years ahead of me. If people are being bullied they should tell someone. I advise you to tell your parents, if not someone very close, then they can bring the matter into school.

The headteacher believes that the PSE work on anti-bullying is 'very much in good order', and the head of Year 11 felt that 'staff commitment has grown because the PSE programme is well structured'. The senior teacher likewise has confidence in 'a PSE programme which has had a maturing influence'. The success of the school's investment in having a teacher as designated counsellor with time allotted for counselling pupils and training peer counsellors is commented on by all staff interviewed. Comments like 'she is motivating and we are lucky to have her', 'the dynamic lead of the school counsellor' and 'she is the inspiration who has steered its impetus with the support of all areas of the school', testify to the value of having a teacher who is given the time and status to focus on the specific issue of bullying. Ofsted acknowledges the usefulness of this role as follows: 'The school counsellor's contribution to the system is effective and highly appreciated by pupils and parents.'

All staff know how the peer counselling service works in detail and see it as a major success. This comment from a newly qualified teacher is typical: 'The pupil counselling system works excellently and indicates that anti-bullying has reached a mature level of success.' Ofsted praises the service as follows:

> The counselling service is exceptionally helpful to pupils. It also provides sixth form counsellors with opportunities to take responsibility for younger pupils.

A tutor referring to comments from some peer counsellors shows the level of their commitment. They told her that 'the work is stressful to them but can also remedy and resolve their own conflicts by talking to others'. She also refers to 'posters everywhere in the corridors and classrooms indicating where help can be obtained and whom to approach. They always include reminders that bullying is not necessarily physical.'

There are various indicators that bullying has been reduced over the last few years. There is a greater willingness for pupils to disclose bullying but it is for less serious incidents. The headteacher and heads of year say there are fewer serious instances reported by pupils and parents. The headteacher says he gets about one complaint a month now compared to once a week a few years ago. The exclusion rates for bullying are very low and comments from the parents at the Ofsted meeting were very favourable.

The senior teacher believes that there is 'far less acceptance that there are victims who are easy meat'. The majority of written comments from pupils affirmed this with statements like: 'I don't think there is a lot of bullying at our school'; 'Most people treat each other well at our school'; 'Our school tries very hard to prevent bullying and is often successful'; 'Pupils think about each other. If one has a problem they can talk about it to a friend and they will mostly keep quiet but try to help'; and 'At our school pupils are pretty cool to each other, this is influenced by the teachers' help.'

The pupils interviewed suggest that bullying incidents are reported on the whole and are dealt with satisfactorily. They each give at least one example of bullying which they had either experienced or witnessed and all except one had been reported to teachers and resolved by them. A Year 9 boy talks about an upsetting break up of a friendship which was resolved after intervention. A Year 11 girl who was in a fight 'defending herself' was pleased with the sensitive support she got from a teacher who resolved the situation for both parties. She also describes how another Year 11 girl was ostracized because she had been 'disloyal' to another regarding a boyfriend. This was not reported, was still continuing uninterrupted and the girl 'has got a reputation now'. A new girl in Year 10 who was verbally abused describes it as 'a nightmare' where she nearly moved schools. This was resolved by the offender being moved by the head of year into another tutor group. A Year 7 pupil was hit with a stool which 'the teacher did not notice and the pupil was too frightened to tell as the offender might beat him up after school'. After another assault by the same pupil he told his parents who informed the teacher and the head of year who then resolved the matter. Some of the pupils' written comments also refer to teachers being 'very supportive' and one referred to a teacher who 'sorted them [a gang of bullies] out'.

Pupils' interviews and written comments show a consistent awareness about the policy and strategies to combat bullying. All those interviewed mention the policy, contract and peer counselling service. They all remember signing the contract and most mention teachers reminding them about it occasionally. One boy refers to talks on bullying about once every six months and knows that the school treats it very seriously. They all think the counsellors are a 'good idea' and as one girl put it, 'they give you the opportunity to vent all your anger'. Several wrote favourable comments about it on the questionnaire along the lines of 'school counselling helps a lot' and 'more schools should have pupil counsellors because this gives upset pupils a chance to talk to another older pupil in confidence and privacy'. There is a sense of their accessibility whereas 'teachers can help but will not always be there'. One girl feels that they are 'probably underused', however.

The pupils' examples of the types of teacher intervention show an awareness of the full variety and how it is 'very variable between staff'.

Most thought teachers would react strongly and consistently, though some incidents were treated more seriously than others and they did not always use the same strategies. Their examples range across: 'dealing with it themselves in class'; 'telling off'; 'lines or detention'; 'isolating offenders'; 'putting them on report'; 'talking to pupils individually'; 'sending pupils individually to counsellors'; 'passing pupils straight to heads of year'; 'sending letters home to parents'; and 'exclusion'. Only the Year 11 girl doubts the effectiveness of school interventions: 'They don't actually solve the problem and they are just a token gesture which sounds good. It normally makes it worse to tell a teacher as they get annoyed.' However, she later gives two examples of teachers helping her and another pupil.

Staff interviews show an awareness of having improved the safety for pupils in the school. The Year 11 head's belief that 'pupils feel safe, they know how to report it and they know something will be done' is a common feeling among the staff but it is offset by comments like 'there is a determination that complacency is to be avoided'.

### Problems

Having the initiatives led by just a few staff members and the pupils has caused some problems. The enthusiasm of the school counsellor and pastoral deputy headteacher, whilst being a driving force behind the policy, may also militate against some teachers taking responsibility for the work. This has not been helped by the lack of whole staff in-service training. The head of Year 11 feels that 'staff commitment has taken some time to establish'. A senior teacher also believes that 'some staff, initially, were not fully committed through a lack of awareness of the size of the possible problem because it's not readily obvious that there is one'. However, the head of Year 7 thinks that, despite the difficulties with staff awareness, acceptance and commitment, 'the battles seem to have been won'.

A significant number of pupils' written comments suggest otherwise, however, and the following criticism is typical of several.

> In our school not enough is done to cut down bullying. If we fight back it is us who get told off for fighting. When teachers see bullying happening in the classroom they don't do anything about it and when you tell them, some will react and sort it out, whereas others will just turn a blind eye and not want to do anything about it. Unless you go to a more concerned member of staff or the counselling service, then nothing is guaranteed to stop.

The pupils' written and spoken comments, whether positive or negative, show a high awareness of the issues which has probably increased during the process of six years' active anti-bullying work. They draw attention to a multitude of bullying behaviours ranging through: 'peer pressure';

'teasing'; 'being really horrible'; 'calling names'; 'a hate letter'; 'talking behind people's backs'; 'verbal fights'; 'taking it out with fists'; 'physical abuse'; bullies being bullied 'by the victim's older brother/sister/friend'; 'bully gangs'; and 'groups who rob individuals'.

The results of this increased awareness have been two-edged. Successes leading to a lower level of pupils' tolerance of bullying are accompanied by an increased workload for teachers in dealing with more disclosures of minor incidents. The headteacher feels a difficulty lies in 'having to make wise judgements. Are children making a fuss or is there a problem? Is it teasing or bullying?' Increased awareness and lower tolerance also seems to have changed the nature of bullying activity and bullies are adopting more subtle forms. The head of Year 7 who feels that 'no school should be complacent', refers to the societal and ability advantages enjoyed by pupils and points out that, 'there are problems nevertheless and they are more subtle'. The head of Year 11 comments on the 'high intelligence trend which can mean that some pupils are clever enough to be subtle in bullying activity and get away with it'. This was felt to be particularly true with verbal bullying, especially among girls, which is more common than physical bullying and often more difficult to detect. Some of the pupils quoted earlier and several written comments exemplify this and it is further confirmed by the relatively high numbers of pupils in the survey reporting being verbally bullied (27 per cent compared to the norm of 24 per cent).

Another potentially subtle type of bullying is when younger pupils bully older pupils. A tutor reports that 'recently a sixth former was bullied by a Year 7 pupil but felt defenceless in terms of retaliation'. She has heard of other Year 7 groups who also targeted sixth formers and wondered how severe the harassment was and whether it was isolated. Also the headteacher is aware of the plight of poorer pupils who are a minority in a school where 'most pupils enjoy a high standard of living'. The previous day he was told by a parent that her child was being teased because he was 'poor'. He points out that 'the few having free school meals can feel in the spotlight as can the less bright'. A pupil's written comment echoes this with:

> you're expected to dress in clothes that are all in fashion all the time and we haven't enough money to. Everyone's got Kickers and we'll never be able to afford any. I get really jealous of really pretty people that have loads of money.

The headteacher wonders

> whether we give youngsters the opportunity to report any distress quickly enough and whether we provide the location points for quick feedback and action. We think we have a range of opportunities but the worry is the odd youngster who doesn't respond and have the matter resolved.

Three of the teachers refer to the competitive ethos of the school which operates alongside a strong pastoral aim to maintain harmonious relationships. The headteacher, aware of the possible tension, feels that the change from a house to a year system has lost some of the competition. He likes to think that, 'celebration has replaced competition', with celebrating each other's successes taking the place of 'winning'. A head of year, however, has noticed that associate teachers, 'always detect a tension caused by high expectations of the pupils' and she feels that the school needs to consider such aspects. A few written comments highlight these kind of pressures on pupils. One wrote, 'I think that younger, less clever, or more clever, pupils are more likely to be bullied', and another, 'I think the most horrible thing that happens to me is that I get called "square" and "perfect" a lot of the time and it is really hurtful.' Another wrote: 'If pupils do something wrong they get teased.'

## The way forward

One pupil's written comments expresses the confidence that although bullying cannot be stopped altogether: 'Greendale do a fairly good job of trying to.' Another emphasizes the idea of self-responsibility:

> You can't control anyone. Some pupils get bullied, it happens everywhere, and for many reasons. All you can do is advise but in the end it's up to us.

Several teachers express a wish to go further than this. The senior teacher sees the need to 'reinforce the realization in pupils' minds that something can be done about bullying' and the head of Year 11 wants to 'keep it going to eliminate bullying altogether'. Pupils interviewed also want to keep up the present policy with the continuation of developing good relationships, counselling and signing of contracts with reminders. One pupil's view that some teachers should be more aware and involved is reflected in several written comments like 'I think some teachers don't listen to both sides'.

The senior teacher's opinion that 'the school needs to build on the fact that its more professional approach to bullying is paying off', seems to reflect the other teachers' views. One year head emphasizes how essential it is to 'keep precise records and review them', and several are keen to follow up the Keele and Years 7 and 8 surveys. The headteacher thinks 'searching for the right data base is important so that good practice can be created and underpin the work already going on at Greendale and elsewhere'. He is especially interested in monitoring gender differences and 'the growing power of girls who are beginning to exercise a powerful influence'. He also wishes 'to review the anti-bullying policy continually' with an incentive allowance being awarded to the teacher in charge. The heads of year feel that the new five-year rotation cycle through the years will make the monitoring of bullying reports easier. Both the headteacher and the newly qualified teacher advocate obtaining information from primary schools regarding bullies and victims.

The school was, according to a senior teacher, initially cautious in 1990 of publicizing its anti-bullying initiatives out of fear of adverse publicity 'as the press were likely to misinterpret so that the school appeared to have a serious bullying problem'. The school now has a policy of making their practice known locally, nationally and internationally. It has also involved other schools in similar projects and in September 1996 it embarked as a leader of the project mentioned earlier. This two-year peer and co-counselling project with Downlands High School and a special school will enable the work to be extended, developed and self-perpetuating when the project is over. The model of Re-evaluation Counselling will enable groups of pupil and staff co-counsellors to meet together in small support groups and joint workshops with other schools thereby challenging the barriers of social class, gender, race and age.

## Conclusion

Oakley, Downlands and Greendale schools, together and individually, show a wide range of successful approaches which have emerged at various stages in each school's individual development. The progress they have made clearly illustrates how anti-bullying work is a multi-level process which involves management as well as curricular issues. Our data suggest that they are all at various points in the early stages of a long process. If the schools are aiming for 'eliminating bullying altogether' a common understanding of their policies, a sharing of their values and a willingness to act by all community members will be crucial.

---

**Reflection**   In each of these case studies there are indications that the staff in the schools are aware of the need for the development of policies and the achievement of their consistent application in the school. What evidence is there that 'core values' need to be developed before any policy can be successful?

---

**TAKING STOCK**

## Introduction

The purpose of the Keele Partnership investigation has been to ascertain the extent of anti-social behaviour within the sample schools and to consider the impact of those policies which have been developed in response to perceived problems. In this chapter, we revisit these themes from both the individual and the institutional viewpoint. Because our study has relied upon the views of pupils currently in the schools, we have no longitudinal perspective except a subjective assessment of the way in which things have changed during their time in the school. However, we have some indication of the nature of change from the comments of staff interviewed in the project. For fourteen of the schools we have the additional material arising from Ofsted inspection reports and assessment of these against pupil and staff comment. The results of the questionnaire survey also enables us to pose some answers to two questions:

- Has increased attention to anti-bullying policies led to an improvement of individual pupil life and the development of self-esteem within the schools?
- Does this make a contribution to the school improvement process?

By inference, we are also able to see whether individual pupils affected by these policies have positive attitudes which they carry into adult society.

## Changes within schools

In the interviews in each school, staff were asked to assess the impact of anti-bullying policies upon the life of the pupils. Staff in seventeen schools showed awareness of the process of monitoring and the evaluation of policies. Four of these schools use questionnaires for some or all of the pupils as the basis of a review of the impact of school policy development either in alternate years for all the school or with specific year groups. The nature of these questionnaires varies from a straightforward simple summary of events based upon the criteria used in the survey of Sheffield schools (Smith and Sharp 1994), to investigations of the full range of school experience of anti-social behaviour and its perceived management based on life in school. Survey construction requires consideration of the following issues. Staff discussion on these topics has been effective in bringing greater cohesion to the corporate view of anti-social behaviour in one of the schools. The use of commercially produced questionnaires such as that offered by Kidscape is being considered in two of the schools.

---

**Points to consider when planning a survey**
- Who is to complete the survey? Every pupil? Certain year groups? A 100 per cent sample or less? For validity it would need to be at least a 25 per cent sample of the group being surveyed.
- If you include the word 'bullying' in the questionnaire, how will you ensure that the pupils will all have the same understanding of what it means?
- Anonymity will increase the validity of the survey. How can confidentiality be guaranteed for every pupil?
- How will you enable pupils who cannot read or write to complete the questionnaires? Older pupils could have one-to-one assistance, perhaps from another pupil or parent.
- Would it be helpful to put bullying behaviour in the context of other behaviour a pupil may have experienced, including pleasant experiences?
- Who will collate the answers and analyse them? It could be a group of sociology pupils or the anti-bullying working party. Outside agencies like local universities, health promotion groups or parent groups may help.

---

Whatever the type of survey used, it will present a snapshot as perceived by the pupils at the time. The maintenance of detailed records of actual reported incidents offers an alternative picture of the reality of life in the school and identifies places, participants and subsequent action. Of the fifteen schools with full interview data, six schools maintain a record of all events but only three use the data to provide year-on-year figures or as a means of identifying vulnerable groups, problem areas and the relationship between bullying or victim experiences and school achievement. The monitoring slip used in one school is reproduced here and, whilst simple in structure, is used by all staff including the lunch-time supervisors and then passed to the year heads for action and subsequent consideration at their team and interyear meetings. This is to ensure that all staff responsible for bully and victim are aware of incidents, but it also contributes to the preparation of statistical analyses.

---

**Greylands High School**

REPORT FORM FOR UNACCEPTABLE BEHAVIOUR

1 What happened?

2 When did it happen?

3 Where were you?

4 Who were you with?

5 Did anyone else see it happen?

6 Any other comments?

Signature ————————————————

Staff signature ————————————————

---

The importance of monitoring and evaluation does not appear to be recognized in twelve of the responding schools. In five of these use is made of formal interstaff communication shown in the following way: 'We have no formal quantitative measure but generally communications are good ... we have regular meetings to discuss pupil progress but bullying is low on the agenda.' For the remaining seven schools, practice varies from 'there is an improved atmosphere with more open pupil–pupil and pupil–staff discussion and I think that staff are more prepared to share problems with other staff than they were' to 'no monitoring is used and I don't think that much bullying ever comes to light'. Possibly more distressing is the situation in those schools where the senior management and the tutors have markedly differing perceptions of monitoring. For example, from five staff in the same school:

No indicators of anti-social behaviour are used, we know that there is a social pressure to become a survivor.

No indicators but we know that some older pupils are showing more responsibility with maturation ... it is really a problem for the town rather than the school.

We only have detail kept for the progress of individuals.

Children begin to have confidence in staff ... the acceptable behaviour of staff is an issue for next year.

School council agenda reflects changes in the concerns of pupils and the head monitors staff for evidence of intimidatory or bullying behaviour.

Where monitoring has been developed the continuing work of an anti-bullying group is significant as a link between existing and future policy. This is demonstrated in one school which has a highly developed policy and a very low incidence of serious problems. The evaluation group considers the annual statistics for parental phone calls, the use of the counsellor and peer counselling systems, the detail provided by year heads and the inclusion of material in curriculum planning. It has conducted two surveys of all pupils in Years 7 and 8 since developing its policy. As a result it is able to adapt policy, for example by developing more consistent record keeping and analysis by the year heads and by 'keeping the staff aware of the issues so that we avoid complacency'.

None of the schools was able to give detailed information of the impact of policies other than in subjective terms. However, eleven of the eighteen schools giving responses consider that some or all of three changes have occurred:

- that there has been a decline of physical bullying in recent years;
- that there has been an increase in taunting and social exclusion; and
- that there has been an increase in the reported involvement of girls in anti-social behaviour.

Charter (1996) offers a national view which shows that these schools are not unusual. Olweus (1994) considers that there was a marked reduction in bully/victim problems within 8–20 months after intervention based upon the modification of pupil behaviour. Peplar *et al.* (1994) trace the changes within schools in Toronto and point to a decline in victimization and fringe bullying involvement within 18 months of intervention. Their survey showed that teachers and pupils were more ready to speak to each other but that there was no significant change in the reporting back to parents. Arora (1994), in an investigation in one secondary school, shows that marked changes of attitude were not sustained until two years after the initial intervention and comments upon the difficulty of securing change in secondary schools – possibly partly related to the developmental stage of pupils, but also to the tendency for staff and parents to be more entrenched in their views and for parents to equate some form of bullying with rites of passage. We certainly gathered evidence of staff resistance to changes which appear to militate against progress and pupil interviews indicate that there is still a degree of bully behaviour by some staff toward pupils and, in two schools, by senior staff toward some junior and female staff. There is a certain hard and court martial feel about the comment that 'every child should have access to three people one to tell them, one to listen to them and one to represent them' and even more so in the view of one junior member of staff that 'some staff believe that there is too much concern about bullying which has been a fact of life for generations'.

There is some concern, however, amongst the staff of schools with whom we have discussed preliminary findings, that the levels of reported bullying appear to have increased in the three schools which have worked most consistently to develop a change of pupil attitude. This accords with the findings reported by Whitney *et al.* (1994) who suggest that awareness of bullying behaviour may lead to increased reporting even though it is declining in severity and overall incidence, and that there may therefore be a negative correlation between effort and outcome. This appears to be true of three schools which have made considerable efforts to develop anti-bullying policies only to find a higher level of reporting of minor nuisance events rather than the serious bullying of former years. We are aware that our questionnaire offered many alternative behaviours without determining the severity of these on some form of scale. The Exeter investigations (Balding *et al.* 1996) allowed respondents to answer according to their own definition of bullying and researchers found that this was more 'physical' than that which had been used in more prescriptive surveys. The success of intervention can only be judged by using the same statistical instrument after a period of time but with changing cohorts of pupils longitudinal measurement is not always easy. For the schools in our sample which have maintained records over a period of time staff say that intervention has been successful in reducing the stress of anti-social behaviour.

## School improvement

This leads to consideration of the link between anti-bullying policies and school improvement. Beare *et al.* (1989) and Stoll and Fink (1996) both consider the necessity for changes in culture as a key to school improvement. Hargreaves and Hopkins (1991) and Hargreaves (1994) develop the processes of institutional planning so that desired aims can be effectively planned for.

The current investigations have shown that anti-bullying policies are important as a means of reinforcing three objectives within the sample schools.

1 Firstly, emphasis on pupil relationships has led the senior staff in schools to consider the ways in which the academic and pastoral curricula can be linked to school objectives. For example, in one school, the anti-bullying programme has been developed as a result of working party investigations of the ways in which teaching can underscore

enhanced interpersonal relationships. This has involved not only the humanities staff but also the teachers of science subjects through class-room organization in practical work.

2  This has led to fulfilment of the second objective, that of securing equal opportunities for racially isolated, educationally disabled and gender groups as outlined by Chazan *et al.* (1994) and by Thompson *et al.* (1994b). Whilst it may be argued that mixed-ability teaching tends to highlight difference between pupils within the same group, there is evidence that support mechanisms may be more readily developed than within discrete setted teaching groups which result in the labelling of whole groups of pupils as 'thick'.

3  Thirdly, the development of anti-bullying approaches has led to some erosion of peer pressure against those who have developed a strong personal work pattern. Evidence from three schools shows that there is an increasing acceptance that 'it is cool to work hard', 'that some people are bright and it helps if you recognize this and work along with them' and 'gradually it seems more important to work if we want to get good results'. The change of attitude can be measured to some extent in the decline of pupil antagonism to the work ethic across the secondary years. Although 17 per cent of Year 7 respondents to the questionnaire felt that 'being too clever' was a reason for taunting and this figure rose to 20 per cent by Year 9, it had declined to 15 per cent by Year 11 and only half the number of respondents in Year 11 (4 per cent) compared with Years 7 and 8, feel that learning difficulties might result in anti-social behaviour.

If these objectives are realized, then school improvement will follow and there is evidence that pupils recognize that where schools are making an effort to overcome bullying other aspects of behaviour are also improving. Of the records of 115 pupil interviews, 78 reflect a view that the staff are generally maintaining a high level of class control and there is praise for those who succeed with this ' because good teachers keep the class in order and spot when there is trouble and act when there is any bullying'. By contrast there is a view that

> some teachers need help so that they keep the classes working . . . one of the best is a teacher who intervened when there was an upset but she did it all without shouting or threats, but some of those who shout at the kids don't get any change, they sort of bully themselves.

There is a contrast between those schools where pupils are not sure to whom they should turn in the event of any difficulty, those where there is a known procedure but little confidence in staff action, and those where known link members of staff are available and are perceived to be effective. This is shown in the proportion of pupils who believe that they would get effective help in each school. For example, in school X which has no written or readily published policy, only 8 per cent of pupils believe that teacher intervention would be helpful; in school Y, with a policy in process of development and a good deal of uncertainty, the percentage rises to 13 per cent (although with caveats in the open comment), but in school Z, with a well-developed policy and a 'view that our pupils watch out for each other', there is a greater confidence in staff with a rise to 28 per cent.

There is an assumption in this that decline in bullying can be equated with an improvement in behaviour. Reid *et al.* (1987) in their consideration of disadvantaged and disaffected pupils suggest that positive relationships and mutual respect between staff and pupils are essential in promoting confidence and self-esteem and that disaffection declines as a result of greater understanding. To this end, they sought more effective training for all staff undertaking pastoral functions, and they commend the importance of whole-school approaches to any improvement strategy. This approach minimizes the risk of subcultures which can subvert the official policy. Hargreaves (1994) offers a model of progression towards improvement from those schools where individualism predominates, characterized by the comment of one pupil that 'the success of what happens in the event of bullying depends on which of the teachers takes any action', through collaboration and contrived collegiality to the 'moving mosaic' where the staff as a whole show flexibility and openness but depend upon consistent planned responses to development objectives. This appears to have influenced the writers of the Ofsted (1995: 61) guidance to those looking at attitudes, behaviour and personal development in the school where

> Pupils' attitudes have a significant bearing on their attainment and progress and can be strongly influenced by what schools do. Good behaviour is vital to productive learning, the quality of life in the school and to the functioning of the school as an orderly community.

Assessment of the success of anti-bullying policies in securing change in schools is dependent upon the context within which it will operate. One of the sample schools has a well-developed policy and indices of the impact of physical mistreatment, verbal taunting and property interference are all low but the narratives show considerable fear about relationships out of school. Another school without such a policy and with a more disadvantaged environment characterized by higher unemployment, older-style housing and a higher proportion of pupils entitled to free meals, has similarly low indices but a greater consistency between life in and out of school. Decker (1995) suggests that this is related to the closeness of the tie between the school and its neighbourhood and that where work with parents underpins what is occurring within the school the culture is more supportive overall. Our evidence suggests that this link can be effective and that there may be some means of measuring the elements in both the anti-bullying policy and the culture of the school so that the relationship between policy, culture and outcomes can be assessed.

## The contribution to school effectiveness

Fourteen of the schools which took part in the survey and which also allowed staff and pupil interviews had also been the subject of Ofsted inspections during the previous two years. The inspection reports have provided additional material for assessment of the impact of anti-bullying approaches through their effect on the culture of the school. Ten of the fourteen schools have written anti-bullying policies and these have also been analysed and scored against a set of criteria based on their potential for effectiveness.

Three features of published policies appear to affect their effectiveness within schools. School respondents may say that they have a policy but in the words of one interviewee 'it is not written because it is part of what we expect from the pupils' and a colleague from the same school suggests that 'there may be a policy but nobody has told me what it is'. The policy may have grown from consideration of issues by all staff and have a high level of 'ownership' but it may have been imposed by management or as a result of a working party conclusion. Interview evidence also shows a great deal of variation in the consistency with which policies are applied and there is a close link between consistency and effectiveness. Consideration of the evidence thus allows classification of schools on the basis of a combination of :

p – a clearly publicized policy
o – a policy developed on a whole-school basis
c – a policy which is consistently applied.

These details are given against the school letter in Table 10.1 It is clear that several schools which do not have anti-bullying policies actually have an overarching behaviour policy which is effective and which presupposes that all anti-social behaviour will be similarly viewed. The head of one such school argued that there is 'only a policy in so far as it operates within a general framework of behaviour and conduct but we look for positive relationships between teachers and pupils and we let the pupils know that all staff will help with any interference'. In another school, the code of conduct includes all breaches of relationships but there is specific anti-bullying teaching through the personal and social education course. However, for the purposes of this analysis, only those schools which have been inspected by Ofsted are included and the information for each allows some judgement on the effectiveness of specific anti-bullying intervention.

**Table 10.1** The relationship between measures of culture and anti-bullying policy effectiveness in a sample of 14 secondary schools

| Policy* | Ofsted 'score' | Physical index | Verbal index | Property index | Ofsted AB comment |
|---|---|---|---|---|---|
| -, -, - | 19 | 5.0 | 19.7 | 6.0 | No mention of policy |
| p, -, c | 20 | 5.1 | 22.3 | 6.0 | Written, operates effectively |
| -, -, - | 20 | 4.2 | 17.5 | 8.3 | Clear code of conduct |
| p, o, c | 21 | 5.1 | 25.7 | 11.9 | Recent, needs monitoring |
| -, -, - | 21 | 5.1 | 27.8 | 7.2 | Pupils uncertain |
| p, -, c | 21 | 3.1 | 8.5 | 3.1 | No mention of policy |
| p, -, - | 24 | 4.0 | 23.6 | 8.5 | No evidence of bullying, staff deal well |
| p, o, c | 24 | 3.3 | 18.8 | 5.3 | Clear code of conduct |
| p, o, c | 26 | 4.2 | 28.3 | 5.7 | No mention of policy |
| p, o, c | 27 | 11.7 | 24.6 | 7.3 | AB policy reinforces positive behaviour |
| p, o, c | 27 | 4.5 | 21.8 | 6.1 | No mention of policy |
| p, -, - | 29 | 9.1 | 22.2 | 7.8 | Detailed policy |
| p, -, c | 30 | 10.4 | 32.1 | 10.6 | Successful bullying charter |
| p, o, c | 31 | 3.7 | 27.5 | 3.7 | Extensive programme |
| Means | 25 | 5.9 | 24.6 | 7.3 | |

* Key:
p indicates a clearly publicized policy.
o indicates that this is on a whole-school basis.
c indicates that there is consistent application of the policy.

The responses from the pupil survey have been analysed to provide a set of indices by considering the reported incidents for each of physical mistreatment, verbal taunting and property damage for each school. The range of 'often' reported physical mistreatment is between 3.0 and 11.7 per cent with a mean of 6.0 per cent; for verbal taunting between 8.5 and 34.9 per cent with a mean of 24.4 per cent, and for interference with property from 3.1 to 11.9 per cent with a mean of 7.1 per cent. However, only 268 reported physical mistreatment and 311 reported property problems, but 1077 reported verbal taunting, by far the most commented upon issue in pupil interviews.

Within the Ofsted reporting system, inspectors have to consider two sets of evidence which are of value in determining aspects of the culture of the school. These are: attitudes, behaviour and personal development; and spiritual, moral, social and cultural development. Together these meet the Beare *et al.* cultural model noted earlier. Comment on the philosophy and operation of equal opportunities policies within the school, and the organization and attitudes shown in the management of pupils with special needs, could also be included in any assessment as a reflection of the school attitudes to vulnerable groups. Ofsted guidance (1995: 60) on the first elements (attitudes, behaviour and personal development) is shown by:

- their attitudes to learning;
- their behaviour, including evidence of exclusions;
- the quality of relationships in the school including the degree of racial harmony where applicable;
- other aspects of their personal development, including their contributions to the life of the community.

The second elements (ibid. 88), spiritual, moral, social and cultural development, is based on the extent to which the school:

- provides its pupils with knowledge and insight into values and beliefs and enables them to reflect on their experiences in a way which develops their spiritual awareness and self-knowledge;
- teaches the principles which distinguish right from wrong;
- encourages pupils to relate positively to others, take responsibility, participate fully in the community, and develop an understanding of citizenship;
- teaches pupils to appreciate their own cultural traditions and the diversity and richness of other cultures.

Inspectors make judgements on these topics after consideration of evidence and then either comment with a degree of criticism, note without comment, or commend what is being done within the school. For the purposes of comparison between the fourteen schools in the present analysis each report was read in detail and graded with a score of 1, if there were elements of criticism, to 3, if the comment was commendatory.

Four elements were noted in each section of the report as follows:

- Behaviour and discipline:
    pupil–pupil, and pupil–staff relationships
    consistent and clear code of conduct
    monitoring and evaluation of incidents
- Spiritual, moral, social and cultural development
    teaching aspects of relationships
    social education and values
    opportunities and involvement on extracurricular activities
- Equal opportunities
    policy development
    organizational strategy
    monitoring and evaluation

- Special needs
    perceptions and policies
    organization and integration
    monitoring and evaluation.

Each of the fourteen reports was analysed according to these criteria and the twelve sections above were each 'scored' 1, 2, 3 to give the Ofsted score in Table 10.1. It is argued that schools with a higher score would be more likely to have a positive culture within which pupils develop than those with a low score where the need for change is indicated by the critical comment. Consideration of the information summarized in Table 10.1 leads to the following conclusions all of which have implications for policymakers in the schools:

- Schools with a positive culture as reflected in the Ofsted score, and a known and effective anti-bullying policy sometimes have high levels of reported anti-social behaviour. This is possibly a reflection of the length of time since the policy was introduced and the more open climate thus engendered although our evidence is that this is a setback for the staff of schools which have made great efforts to secure improvement.
- Schools with a positive culture but no specific anti-bullying policy appear to have lower indices of reported incidents. However, they also score below the mean on the Ofsted rating. This suggests that the reality of personal relationships and the cultural environment may be adverse and lead to a low level of reporting because of fear of reprisal.
- Schools with an Ofsted score below the mean are less likely to have specific anti-bullying policies. This may indicate that concern with the improvement of that culture could lead to an investigation of the dynamics of group activities and relationships.
- Schools which have developed clear anti-bullying policies, fully owned by the staff and consistently applied are more likely to have a positive general culture. The transition from policy to practice is believed to be fundamental to long-term improvement.
- The evidence from the fourteen schools in this sample is inconclusive as an indicator of the effectiveness of anti-bullying policies. This is a reflection of the level of awareness of what constitutes anti-social behaviour, the level of reporting and the staff attitudes in the schools concerned. In general, the greater the awareness and the more open the context the greater is the likelihood of reported behaviour. For these schools the effectiveness of policies may perhaps be better judged by the Ofsted score rather than by survey responses.

Evidence from the questionnaire responses for all 25 schools also enables a comparison between those schools which have written policies and those which rely upon a set of social values embedded in the general ethos of the school. There is little difference between the level of response for the schools with and those without policies as shown in that both have about 70 per cent of pupils reporting one or more physical taunts in the past year and both have 32 per cent of pupils reporting some property damage. However, the impact of policies in beginning to secure improvement can be seen in that only 76 per cent report an incident of verbal taunts in those schools with policies and 81 per cent report similarly in schools without policies – 'relationships are more human'. Caution is needed in the interpretation of these data – one or more incidents gives no indication of overall incidence or of the comparative severity of anti-social behaviour in different schools.

In short, whilst there is a strong relationship between a positive culture and effective anti-bullying policies, the existence of an anti-bullying policy without contextual support is likely to be less effective in establishing a positive social environment. This can be demonstrated in the almost automatic use of suspension as a sanction against bullies. In twelve of the schools there is a known, staged, system which leads to fixed exclusion for serious and repeated anti-social behaviour and the pupils who were interviewed appear to support this as a means of dealing with persistent troublemakers. They doubted whether it made any long-term difference in three of the schools which have high levels of exclusion as a result of the automatic nature of the progression of sanctions. Indeed, one pupil comments that

> if the case is serious then the pupils should be permanently excluded and refused access to the school afterwards, irrelevant [sic] to the amount of grovelling done by irresponsible parents who should have conducted more discipline to the child at a younger age.

Two of the schools have alternative approaches which do rather more to meet the needs of the participants in any dispute. One counsels both bully and victim with a modified 'no blame' approach but seeking redress from the bully, and the other by having a monitoring meeting each week between the bully, the year head and the pastoral deputy head which is 'insistent and investigative but keeps things at the lowest profile possible'.

The evidence suggests that the emphasis must then shift to cultural as opposed simply to policy controls on pupil development. These are identified in part by the responses in pupil interviews when they were asked to explain what they considered to be an ideal intervention to overcome any aggressive behaviour. These are shown in Table 10.2 and suggest that pupils are more ready to change the context within which relationships develop than to work on specific programmes to overcome bullying. If this is so, then anti-bullying may be approached as an integral part of the broader ethos of the school.

**Table 10.2** Ideal interventions to overcome aggressive behaviour ($n$ = 115 pupils)

| Intervention | Male responses | Female responses | Total |
|---|---|---|---|
| Anti-bullying contract | 2 | 2 | 4 |
| Anti-bullying committee | 2 | 4 | 6 |
| Counselling | 2 | 7 | 9 |
| Sanctions | 9 | 5 | 14 |
| School aims link | 6 | 4 | 10 |
| Personal and social education link | 7 | 5 | 12 |
| Action against external groups | 1 | 2 | 3 |
| Extramural activities | 9 | 2 | 11 |
| Policy reminders | 9 | 9 | 18 |
| Teachers talking and observing | 11 | 8 | 19 |
| Developing friendship groups | 20 | 8 | 28 |

## Anti-bullying and the culture of the school

The assumption that anti-bullying strategies are likely to be more success-ful if they are part of a positive school culture is fundamental to whole school policy development as explored in recent investigations such as Smith and Sharp (1994: 65) who contend that 'Effective policy develop-ment depends upon thorough consultation'. Tattum *et al.* (1993) conclude that the work is part of the provision of a supportive, safe and secure learn-ing environment and Mulhern (1994) who argues that anti-bullying is but part of the general tenor of life in a school. Three of the schools which we have investigated believe that separate treatment of anti-bullying is likely to be less important than the encouragement of an overall and positive code of behaviour, and seven have developed anti-bullying as an offshoot of investigations of pupil–pupil and pupil–staff relationships. This sug-gests that there may be schools within which an anti-bullying policy is more easily developed than in others. The atmosphere within the school can accord with one of the following:

*positive* – where staff are prepared to listen, where pupils are ready to co-operate with planned changes which may be to their advantage, and where parents and community endeavour to extend the support beyond the school;

*neutral* – where staff act in a pragmatic way to contain any difficulty, where pupils follow the rules but have their own set of conventions when out of sight of staff, and where parents and community leave the school to act in isolation; and

*adverse* – where staff act only in crisis situations, where pupils frequently challenge rules and have their own intergroup code of conduct, and where parents and community speak in terms of resolution of problems through conflict.

Two vignettes, drawn from sample schools, are illustrated here.

---

**Rivermead School**

A positive situation is demonstrated in this school where a well-developed code of conduct has been used as a peg upon which to hang a bullying charter and its attendant responsibilities for staff and pupils. Sanctions are sparingly used and rewards, together with a move to assertive discipline, are resulting in an open discussion of issues which staff would formerly have seen as 'weakness', and a consequent attempt to secure consistency in staff approaches to problems. Pupil involvement through pastoral and linked curriculum work has been encouraged further by participative structures and lively school council work. Parental support is very strong and their involvement in policymaking has been encouraged and moves are under way to involve external agencies in a school linked community provision.

---

**Longmeadow School**

This school serves a disadvantaged neighbourhood with a long history of antipathy from parents who blame their own problems on an inadequate school experience. Some of the staff at the school were known to the parents in the secondary modern phase and have a reputation to sustain as being 'hard', but fair, within the constraints of a tough neighbourhood. This group of staff is fearful of giving any power to the pupils or of being seen to be soft and as a result feel that encouragement to pupils to tell in any way would weaken the disciplinary hold of the school. There is little overt bullying and when it is apparent it is dealt with through temporary exclusion of the bully – as a result there is a feeling amongst some staff that no problems exist for pupils. The situation is worsened by the tensions between the 'traditional' staff and newly appointed colleagues who favour a more open approach, especially where they are form tutors of underachieving youngsters, many of whom are subject to harshness at home and bullying at school. The attitude of external agencies is to undertake crisis intervention with families and to maintain order but there is little school–agency communication. Nevertheless, the school is seen by parents as an orderly community with little evidence of indiscipline, and it is recognized as caring for the pupils.

## Intervention for the individual

The impact of anti-bullying policies may affect the culture of the school as an organization but the perceived impact on individual pupils is a significant outcome upon which success will be judged. In the questionnaire, pupils were asked to assess the change arising from teacher intervention and in the interviews the process of intervention was investigated in relation to narratives discussed with the pupils. Teachers were acknowledged as managing anti-bullying in five ways:

- through crisis intervention following actual events;
- through action with bullies and victims by staff and peers over a longer period;
- through the application of a hierarchy of sanctions;
- through assemblies, personal and social education, and tutorial work; and
- by the use of shared value systems based on the way things are done in the school.

The main thrust of anti-bullying polices has been to encourage pupils to tell somebody in authority about any incidents so that action can be taken to suppress anti-social behaviours. The immediate response to threats or physical hurt is to stand up to the aggressor (54 per cent of questionnaire respondents) and then to tell somebody (37 per cent). However, this masks a gender difference in that boys will be more ready to respond with a fight but girls will be more ready to tell a member of staff, perhaps because they feel that they will get a more sympathetic hearing. The younger pupils are more ready to tell but the older ones clearly take the law into their own hands and are twice as ready to fight at Year 11 than in Year 7. This is acknowledged as a result of 'being older and more ready to stick up for yourself' and of 'getting something done without the bother of having teachers involved'. In a multi-option response, it is disturbing that 16 per cent would suffer and keep quiet and that 24 per cent would simply avoid the location where trouble occurs.

When telling someone is followed as a precept the best friend is the most common source of help in school (61 per cent), with the form tutor as the most significant authority figure (26 per cent), and mother as the most often turned-to parent (44 per cent). Respondents believe that teachers would, however, act differently according to the situation and the reason for the bullying activity. Racism, religion, learning difficulties, and disability would, pupils think, be treated seriously by more than three-quarters of the staff but this may be because they are topics which form part of the personal and social education or tutorial discussion in most schools. Being new to the school appears to be very well supported by staff as needing quick intervention and support in any reported incident.

Matters of gender, size, looks, family background, speech, being different, and work habits fall into a group which would be helped for about half the time. Matters of finance, dress, cleverness and sporting prowess form a group of causes of incidents which may be supported by less than half the staff approached. This may add weight to the interview comments that 'sometimes the teachers side with the bullies – they believe what they are saying' and 'the comments of teachers, especially when they laugh at what you are saying, only make matters worse'.

Up to 8 per cent of pupils believe that at some point they would be told to 'stop telling tales' and up to 13 per cent believe that teachers would not be interested. In so far as there is a ranking of perceived intervention for physical bullying, pupils believe that 90 per cent of teachers would act if violence was threatened or if there was a complaint of a sexual nature, but only 73 per cent of teachers would act over slapping, 59 per cent of teachers would act over hair-pulling, and 52 per cent over complaints of tripping and pushing. As these are the most frequently reported physical incidents against girls this may go some way to explain why 4 per cent less girls think that teacher intervention is a help. The overall effectiveness of teacher action is regarded as positive by just over half of the pupils. This was investigated further in the interviews. The responses for the full range of possible interventions on behalf of an individual in difficulty in the school are summarized in Table 10.3. The responses here are not mutually exclusive, but most pupils spoke of the person intervening and the type of intervention used.

These responses show the importance of teachers as the main source of intervention and of sanctions as the main tactic for securing improvement. Problems occur when intervention follows 'grassing' in any form. This

**Table 10.3** Effectiveness of staff intervention listed by pupils interviewed (*n* = 115 pupils)

| Intervention | Intervention helps | | Intervention causes problems | |
|---|---|---|---|---|
| | Boys | Girls | Boys | Girls |
| Teachers | 11 | 6 | 17 | 21 |
| Senior staff | 1 | 4 | 1 | 2 |
| Police | 3 | 0 | 3 | 2 |
| Parents | 2 | 0 | 1 | 1 |
| Peers | 2 | 2 | 3 | 1 |
| Known policies | 7 | 3 | 2 | 0 |
| Sanctions | 15 | 8 | 8 | 2 |
| Changed values | 15 | 8 | 11 | 3 |
| PSE tutorials | 1 | 1 | 4 | 3 |
| Assemblies | 4 | 2 | 6 | 5 |

was mentioned by 33 per cent of the interviewed pupils but only by 23 per cent of those answering the questionnaire – perhaps a reflection of the heightened awareness of the reason for the investigation in the interviews. Overall only 14 of the 115 interviewed believe that there is an improvement and 41 believe that things get worse. In response to this question, interviewees suggest that in 11 narratives teachers intimidated, embarrassed or broke confidentiality to the detriment of the victim. Whatever the source of evidence there is concern that over 50 per cent of teacher intervention in the investigation overall is perceived as of limited effect. Open comments yielded evidence of what a pupil sees as mishandled help, and what pupils seek in ideal teacher intervention:

> A boy a couple of years older than me pulled a flick knife out on me. He didn't harm me with it, he just ran off. I reported the incident straight away but nothing was done about it. Eventually my dad came up to the school and because of this I had to give a full identification of the boy because I did not know his name. A group of boys were collected together and I had to identify him.

> I think that teachers should put across to pupils more that they are there to help and if anyone needs to talk to them they must feel free to do so because I think that if pupils are being bullied they may be too shy to say anything. If a teacher suspects a pupil is being bullied I think that the teacher should approach the pupil and make it clear that they are there to talk if they need to do so.

The reverse is seen in comments where teachers appear to be inept or fail to explain their intervention more clearly to those involved:

> I feel that there is far too much bullying at school and that teachers can't be bothered so it ends up either getting so bad your parents take it into their own hands or often go to the extent of involving the police.

> I find when going to a teacher they either don't believe you or take somebody else's side . . . I don't go to teachers any more it just makes it worse and you end up in more trouble.

There is evidence that action is taken against bullies but that the school at large and the victim in particular, may not get to know what has happened. Whilst the sanctions are known and questionnaire responses indicate that 48 per cent believe that aggressors would be punished in school, and 37 per cent believe that they would be excluded, there is also a belief by 36 per cent that parents would be summoned to the school but not necessarily as a sanction. However, 27 per cent believe that telling off has no effect, 17 per cent that things will get worse and 9 per cent that nothing will happen. The fundamental misunderstanding here though is that the confidentiality which the victim seeks is also accorded to the bully in most school policies, and good counselling requires that this should be so. To accord with the Children Act 1989, teachers acting in a counselling role can only guarantee confidentiality if in doing so there would be no serious risk to the pupil.

It is not only the intervention but also the curriculum emphasis on tolerance and the avoidance of anti-social behaviour which is noted by the interviewees and in open comment. There is a definite variation between schools in this area of the investigation. In two schools, all the pupils spoke at some point of the programmes of discussion, of the shared values which were part of assemblies and tutorial work and of the value of the anti-bullying contract and some form of counselling support. In eleven schools, there is some reference to each of these at some point in the interviews and in three others pupils only speak about assemblies, PSE and varied teacher attitudes. Comments may be positive reflecting 'good discussion', 'enjoyed the role play', 'learning about tolerance to other people' and 'we learnt how to help other people who were in trouble'. At the other extreme, there is pupil comment on 'doing a worksheet about racism', 'PSE is when there is a lot of mucking about', 'not very interested' and 'we have a bullying contract but we need to be reminded of this every term'.

## Towards policy development

The two vignettes and the perceptions of pupils demonstrate the variety of contexts within which anti-bullying policies have been developed and the interaction of organization and individual. This leads to the view that pupils will only benefit where there is open discussion of a number of issues. The audit stage requires carefully structured surveys to determine the nature of reality in a given situation (Mellor 1995). The planning stage requires the involvement of all parties to consider both the rationale for action and the content of policy. Mason (1993) has demonstrated that this can only be successful within an already open and effective pastoral system which has determined basic values for the school. Implementation is only successful if all staff are committed and consistent (Stoll and Fink 1996), and continuing monitoring and evaluation are necessary if the impact of a policy is not to be lost. Our evidence is that both the process of data collection and the analysis of events requires considerable staff training, especially where counselling has taken place (Randall 1996). All these, however, affect all stakeholders within and beyond the school and the policy has to address the concerns of each group.

### The individual

Our evidence demonstrates that anti-bullying policies, whilst possibly reducing physical violence, are not yet effective in reducing the misery for some pupils which arises from frequent verbal taunting and interference with property. Nolin (1995) outlines the way in which the invasion of liberty – by constraining freedom of action, of space, by leading pupils to develop avoidance strategies and of the right to social and educational development, through impaired classroom opportunities – are affecting up to 10 per cent of a complete cohort of young people in the USA each year. Our figures show a similar problem in the sample schools. The most difficult problems are those relating to the development of self-esteem in those pupils who are under constant pressure and become either bully/victims, or passive victims and lack the necessary assertiveness and problem-solving skills to cope with social interaction except from a position of insecurity. Successful policies do not stereotype either bully or victim but build upon individual needs through counselling support (Barletta 1995). In a period of financial retrenchment schools lack the resources to finance such work and where individual work may not be possible group activities are being increasingly used.

## Group activities

The twofold aim of most group-based activity is to encourage positive social attitudes and develop group skills. This may be through curriculum and social activity opportunities such as those outlined by Tattum and Herbert (1993) and through student self-help and peer counselling as outlined by Cowie and Sharp (1995), but it may also be fostered through positive attitudes to those problems which affect groups in the school and especially the issue of gang membership. Our evidence suggests that involvement is seen as a mirror of social groupings out of school, and for some pupils it offers a bridge between school and the local late adolescent community. Within school, staff watchfulness to prevent erosion of the liberty of some through 'no go' areas established by others, and to counterintimidation through the influence of power groups within the social structure of the school appear essential. Wilczenski (1994) has demonstrated that a link can be made between individual experience as bully and victim and group socio-drama activities extending the ideas to group interaction. Changing the attitudes of groups is not easy unless it is part of a concerted school policy and whilst Squires and Kranyik (1995) have shown that cultural change within schools is probably more effective than concentrating on individual pupil development, the achievement of change may be much more difficult given the complexity of group dynamics.

## The school

The varied experience of those schools which have adopted anti-bullying policies indicates that the most significant factor in securing change is the encouragement given by all staff to whole-school development. This may be through participation in the enforcement of a set of procedures, through the use of curriculum opportunities or through reinforcement of principles and the ethos of the school as set out by Tattum *et al.* (1993). It may also arise through willingness to participate in monitoring, e.g. as in the use of intervention videos described by Boulton and Flemington (1996), and in discussion which builds upon the evaluation of existing policies. Problems arise, though, in the lack of available time for the investigation, counselling and support of those pupils who are in need of help. There are also comments from staff about the difficulties of working within the constraints of current legislation and the fear of censure or litigation should well-meaning support be misinterpreted. In this respect, the development of 'full service' schools in the USA is fostering a more accessible set of support agencies to work alongside, or to take on, the work of the teaching professionals in building links between school and home (Dryfoos 1995). The current situation is described by one member of staff as 'having to take on the woes of society as our mistakes, and then find the time to do our real work' but the schools providing evidence of successful anti-bullying policies have developed systems which minimize intrusion into teaching and a more positive comment from one form tutor offers hope:

> It took a while to get used to new ways of thinking and to dealing with the youngsters in a way which seemed soft, but we have now minimized the problems and the reduction in the number of serious incidents within a better climate has paid off . . . it is all much more positive.

## The community

There is considerable difficulty in working with the diverse neighbourhoods from which the pupils at any one school may come and the direct relationship between school and community has been lessened for two-thirds of the schools in our sample. Problems have been exacerbated where former community agencies have been removed in response to local education authority financial pressures and the schools can no longer sustain community liaison staff. Much of our investigation has hinged on the interplay between the school and the community in securing a change of attitudes and we have suggested that there are occasions when a clash between the culture of home and neighbourhood, and the ethos of the school, results in misunderstanding rather than the promotion of supportive harmony. Decker (1995) refers to these as the forces of resistance and outlines strategies including home visiting, group activities and the incorporation of parents in school-based work. The interviews which have underpinned much of our thinking have shown that there is a willingness to build bridges but it is hampered in many secondary schools by the distance between the school and the neighbourhoods it serves, by the element of competition which means that several schools may serve an area, and by the limited time which teachers have for community involvement – even if, and this is by no means certain, it would be welcomed. The interventions considered by the survey respondents included staff from school, parents and family and friends, older pupils and people beyond these groups. Whilst 15 per cent would seek help from somebody in the community the strength of the peer group as an influence is shown in the fact that 61 per cent would seek help from their best friend. This suggests that the concentration of effort on individual, group and school activities is more likely to provide value for money than work in the community. However, the development of a sympathetic environment seems an essential prerequisite for a changed culture. The removal of barriers to understanding may require intervention at a national level to raise awareness and develop a partnership between schools and the community at large. The fear is that media attention to violence and failure (MacDougal 1993) may inhibit the efforts of those who can demonstrate that the lives of pupils are improving because of efforts being made in classroom and school to change the fundamental values of those who engage in all forms of taunting behaviour. Policy development does, however, require underscoring by the community if it is to be successful – changing views of telling, retaliating, and acceptable adolescent values require new strategies on a wider front than schools alone can sustain.

## Conclusion

Although there continue to be considerable problems in relationships between pupils in our schools the Keele research has shown four positive trends:

1 Schools are increasingly aware of the need for action against anti-social behaviour.
2 There has been some decrease in the incidence of serious and repeated acts of physical bullying.
3 There is evidence that most pupils want a better school society and are attempting to achieve this – 75 per cent of respondents feel 'ashamed when someone has been hurt'.
4 Staff in schools are working towards shared value systems which recognize individual rights to equality of opportunity.

Even so, we find that overall about one-fifth of pupils in the schools we worked with, i.e. 900 pupils, still find always or mostly that 'it's tough being me', 'I have a low opinion of myself' and 'people tell lies about me'.

About one-tenth are teased or excluded from social groupings, and one-twentieth suffer physical hurt and/or property damage 'often or very often'. Schools are increasingly aware of these problems and we have been privileged to share their approaches to an improved environment for all pupils.

Part of the problem, however, lies beyond the school. Recent educational policy has strengthened the market imperative through greater emphasis on parental choice with increasing elements of selection and competition between schools. This may reinforce the sense of exclusion which is felt by pupils who see themselves as attending a second choice school, or who feel that they cannot aspire to those qualities which are commended in a school driven by the need to perform well in the league tables. Where changed culture depends on the effectiveness of the link between school and community but the community has become more diffuse and resistant, barriers between the school and its environment inhibit progress. The introduction of successful policies may be hampered because of the poor definition of the community and a lack of vision of what might be for an area. This has been accelerated where former local education authority funding is not as readily available either within the community or within the schools. The diminution of support for special needs pupils in the mainstream of schools, and the lack of help from support agencies either for pre-school or excluded pupils, is increasing the vulnerability of those most at risk. It seems that the hoped for changes in attitude one to another within schools can only be achieved when society also accepts the twin challenges to recognize differences of background, wealth and aspirations, and to support those who feel that they lack self-esteem and the opportunity for success in life. 'Being different' lies at the heart of the problems experienced by many pupils, both the victims who are taunted because they are not understood by others, and the bullies who are aggressive because they cannot match their peers in other ways. Our evidence is that many schools are tackling this problem as one of a number of competing priorities against a background of limited home and community support.

# BIBLIOGRAPHY

Adler, M., Petch, A. and Tweedie, J. (1989) *Parental Choice and Educational Policy*. Edinburgh: Edinburgh University Press.

Ahmad, Y. and Smith, P.K. (1990) Bullying in schools and the issue of sex differences. *Newsletter for Association of Child Psychology and Psychiatry*, 12: 44–7.

Ahmad, Y., Whitney, I. and Smith, P. (1991) A survey service for schools on bully/victim problems, in P.K. Smith and D.A. Thompson (eds) *Practical Approaches to Bullying*. London: David Fulton.

Arora, C.M.J. (1994) Is there any point in trying to reduce bullying in secondary schools? *Educational Psychology in Practice*, 10(3): 155–62.

Arora, C.M.J. and Thompson, D.A. (1987) Defining bullying for a secondary school. *Education and Child Psychology*, 4: 110–20.

Balding, J., Regis, D., Wise, A., Bish, D. and Muirden, J. (1996) *Bully Off: Young people that fear going to school*. Exeter: School Health Education Unit, University of Exeter.

Barletta, J. (1995) *Legal and Ethical Issues for School Counsellors: Supervision as a safeguard*. Cleveland OH: Counseling and Personnel Services.

Batsche, G.M. and Knoff, H.M. (1994) Bullies and their victims: understanding a pervasive problem in schools. *School Psychology Review*, 23(2): 165–74.

Beare, H., Caldwell, B. and Millikan, R.H. (1989) *Creating an Excellent School*. London: Routledge.

Bentley, K.M. and Li, A.K. (1995) Bully and victim problems in elementary school districts and students' beliefs about aggression. *Canadian Journal of School Psychology*, 11(2): 153–65.

Berndt, T.J. (1992) Deflating peer pressure. *Science News*, November 14, 142(20): 331.

Besag, V. (1989) *Bullies and Victims in Schools*. Milton Keynes: Open University Press.

Besag, V. (1992) *We Don't Have Bullies Here*. Privately published, 57 Manor House Road, Jesmond, Newcastle-upon-Tyne.

Blatchford, P. (1993) Bullying in the playground environment, in D. Tattum (ed.) *Understanding and Managing Bullying*. London: Heinemann.

Boulton, M. (1993) Proximate causes of aggressive fighting in middle school children. *British Journal of Educational Psychology*, 63: 231–44.

Boulton, M. (1994) Playground behaviour and peer interaction patterns of primary school boys classified as bullies, victims and not involved. *British Journal of Educational Psychology*, 65: 11–23.

Boulton, M. and Flemington, I. (1996) The effects of short video intervention on secondary school pupils' involvement in, definitions of, and attitudes towards, bullying. *School Psychology International*, 17: 331–45.

Boulton, M. and Underwood, K. (1992) Bully/victim problems among middle school children. *British Journal of Educational Psychology*, 62: 73–87.

Bowe, R. and Ball, S. (1992) *Reforming Education and Changing Schools*. London: Routledge.

Brimblecombe, N., Shaw, M. and Ormston, M. (1996) Teachers' intentions to change practice as a result of OFSTED school inspections. *Educational Management and Administration*, 24(4): 339–54.

Byrne, B. (1994a) Bullies and victims in a school setting. *Irish Journal of Psychology*, 15(4): 574–86.

Byrne, B. (1994b) *Bullying – A Community Approach*. Dublin: The Columba Press.

Carlen, P., Gleeson, D. and Wardhaugh, J. (1992) *Truancy: The politics of compulsory schooling*. Buckingham: Open University Press.

Carter, S. (1994) *Prevention: Organising systems to support competent social behaviour in children and youth*. Washington, OR: Office of Special Education.

Cartwright, N. (1995) Combatting bullying in school: the role of peer helpers, in H. Cowie and S. Sharp (eds) *Peer Counselling in Schools*. London: David Fulton.

Chambliss, W.J. (1995) Crime control and ethnic minorities; legitimizing racial oppression by creating moral panics, in D.F. Hawkins (ed.) *Ethnicity, Race and Crime: Perspectives across time and place*. Albany NY: State University Press.

Chandler, K. (1995) *Student Strategies to Avoid Harm at School: Statistics in brief*. Washington DC: National Center for Educational Statistics.

Charter, D. (1996) One third of girls are afraid of being bullied. *The Times*, 29 June 1996.

Chazan, M., Laing, A.F. and Davies, D. (1994) *Emotional and Behavioural Difficulties in Middle Childhood: Identification, assessment and intervention in school*. London: Falmer Press.

Cicourel, A.V. (1995) *The Social Organisation of Juvenile Justice*. New Brunswick: Transaction Publications.

Compton, D. and Baizerman, M. (1991) Services for students at risk in schools; would more be better and is better good enough? *Children To-day*, 20(1): 8–12.

Cowie, H. and Sharp, S. (1992) Students themselves tackle the problem of bullying. *Pastoral Care in Education*, 10(4): 31–7.

Cowie, H. and Sharp, S. (1994) Tackling bullying through the curriculum, in P.K. Smith and S. Sharp (eds) *School Bullying: Insights and perspectives*. London: Routledge.

Cowie, H. and Sharp, S. (1995) *Peer Counselling in Schools*. London: David Fulton.

Cutright, P. (1995) Neighbourhood social structure and the lives of black and white children. *Sociological Focus*, 27(3): 243–55.

Dalin, P. (1993) *Changing the School Culture*. London: Cassell.

Davis, V. (1996) The early experiences of OFSTED, in J. Ouston, P. Earley and B. Fidler (eds) *OFSTED Inspections: The early experience*. London: David Fulton.

de Acosta, M. (1994) *Reconsidering the role of community in home-school links: Implications for research and practice. Occasional paper 14*. Cleveland OH: State University.

Decker, L.E. (1995) *Parent and Community Involvement. Field Review Edition*. Boca Raton FL: Atlantic University.

Department of Education and Science (1989) *Discipline in Schools: Report of the committee chaired by Lord Elton*. London: HMSO.

Department for Education (1994) *Bullying: don't suffer in silence*. London: HMSO.

Downey, G. and Coyne, J.C. (1990) Children of depressed parents: an integrative review. *Psychological Bulletin*, 108: 50–76.

Drouet, D. (1993) Adolescent female bullying and sexual harassment, in D.Tattum (ed.) *Understanding and Managing Bullying*. London: Heinemann.

Dryfoos, J.G. (1995) Full service schools; schools and community based organisations finally get together to address the crisis in disadvantaged communities. *Educational Leadership*, 53(7): 18–23.

Dymond, P. and Gilmore, J. (1993) *The Listening School: Creating a preventative curriculum*, Shropshire: Links, Pontesbury.

Elliot, M. (1986) *A Booklet for Parents and Material for Teachers*. London: Kidscape.

Erwin, D. (1995) *Improving School Climate and Strengthening Relationships Amongst the School Community*. Chicago IL: State University.

Evans, D. (1994) *Student Behaviour Problems: Positive initiatives and new frontiers*. Melbourne, Victoria: Australian Centre for Educational Research.

Fertman, C. (1993) Creating successful collaborations between schools and community agencies. *Children To-day*, 22(2): 32–4.

Fieldman, G., Chang, H. and Leong, C. (1992) The community connection. *California Perspectives*, Autumn. San Francisco CA: Fort Mason Center.

Frank, D. and Rocks, W. (1996) Exploiting instability: a model for managing organisational change. *Annual International Conference of the National Community College Chair Academy, Phoenix, Arizona*, February 14–17.

Fullan, M.G. (1991) *The New Meaning of Educational Change*. London: Cassell.

Galloway, D. (1985) Pastoral care and school effectiveness, in D. Reynolds (ed.) *Studying School Effectiveness*. London: Falmer Press.

Galloway, D. (1994) Bullying: the importance of a whole-school approach. *Therapeutic Care and Education*, 3(1): 19–26.

Garrity, C. (1994) Bully proofing your school – a comprehensive elementary curriculum. *Safe Schools Conference*, Washington DC, October 28–29.

Gleeson, D. (1994) Wagging, bobbing and bunking off: an alternative view. *Educational Review*, 46(1): 15–19.

Glover, D.C. (1992) An investigation of criteria used by parents and community in judgement of school quality. *Educational Research*, 34(1): 35–44.

Glover, D.C., Bennett, N., Levacic, R. and Earley, P. (1996) Leadership, planning and resource management in four very effective schools. Parts 1 and 2. *School Organisation*, 16(2,3): 135–48, 247–61.

Glover, D.C., Gough, G. and Johnson, M. (1997) What the parents think . . . bullying. *Managing Schools To-day*, 6(4): 36.

Gordon, P. (1992) Racial incidents in Britain, 1988–90: a survey. *Runnymede Bulletin*, number 254.

Hammond, T. and Dennison, B. (1995) School choice in less populated areas. *Educational Management and Administration*, 23(2): 104–13.

Hargreaves, A. (1994) *Changing Teachers, Changing Times: Teachers' work and culture in the postmodern age*. London: Cassell.

Hargreaves, D. (1995) School culture, school effectiveness and school improvement. *School Effectiveness and School Improvement*, 6(1): 23–46.

Hargreaves, D. and Hopkins, D. (1991) *The Empowered School: The management and practice of development planning*. London: Cassell.

Hazler, R.J. (1994) Bullying breeds violence. *Learning*, 22(6): 38–41.

Higgins, C. (1994) Improving the school ground environment as an anti-bullying intervention, in P.K. Smith and S. Sharp (eds) *School Bullying: Insights and perspectives*. London: Routledge.

Holmes, G.R. (1995) *Teenagers into Adulthood: A guide for the next generation*. Westport CT: Greenwood.

Home Office (1995) *Preventing School Bullying*. London: Police Research Group, Home Office.

Hoover, J.H. (1993) Perceived victimisation by school bullies; new research and future directions. *Journal of Humanistic Education and Development*, 32(2): 76–84.

Hoover, J.H. and Juul, K. (1993) Bullying in Europe and USA. *Journal of Emotional and Behavioural Problems*, 2(1): 25–9.

Humphrey, K. and Baker, P.R. (1994) The GREAT programme; gang resistance, education and training. *FBI Law Enforcement Bulletin*, 63(9): 1–5.

Hunter, J.B. (1991) Which school? A case study of parents'choice of secondary school. *Educational Research*, 33(1): 22–30.

Jones, P. (1994) Boys will be boys: does this explain pupils' experience of bullying in a mixed comprehensive school? *Pastoral Care in Education*, 12(3): 3–10.

Karpicke, H. and Murphy, M.E. (1996) Productive school culture: principals working from the inside. *National Association of Secondary School Principals Bulletin*, 80, 576.

Kelly, E. and Cohn, T. (1988) *Racism in Schools: New research evidence*. Stoke-on-Trent: Trentham Books.

Kenny, M. (1995) Whatever happened to the stiff upper lip? *Sunday Telegraph*, 1 November 1995.

La Fontaine, J. (1991) *Bullying: The child's view*. London: Calouste Gulbenkian Foundation.

Levine, K. (1993) The meaning of mean. *Parents Magazine*, 68(8): 98–102.

Lister, P. (1995) Bullies, the big new problem you must know about. *Redbook*, 186(1): 116–22.

Loach, B. and Bloor, C. (1994) Dropping the bully to find the racist. *Multicultural Teaching*, 13(2): 18–20.

Lowenstein, L.F. (1978a) The bullied and the non-bullied child. *Bulletin of British Psychological Society*, 31: 316–18.

Lowenstein, L.F. (1978b) Who is the bully? *Bulletin of British Psychological Society*, 31: 147–49.

MacDougal, J. (1993) *Violence in the schools: programmes and policies for prevention. A report from the Canadian Education Association*. Toronto: Canadian Education Association.

McNamara, C. (1995) A school policy against bullying: evolution, not intervention. *Pastoral Care in Education*, 13 September: 3–6.

Marano, H.E. (1995) Big bad bully. *Psychology To-day*, 28(5): 50–68.

Marston, P. (1996) Parents call for tougher policies on bullying. *Daily Telegraph*, 28 March 1996.

Martin, J. and Meyerson, D. (1988) Organisational culture and the denial, channeling and acknowledgement of ambiguity, in L. Pandy, R.J. Boland and H. Thomas (eds) *Managing Ambiguity and Change*. New York: John Wiley.

Mason, A. (1993) Management strategies. 4. Wycliffe College, in D. Tattum and G. Herbert (eds) *Countering Bullying – Initiatives by schools and local authorities*. Stoke-on-Trent: Trentham Books.

Maynard, R. (1993) Bullying: how parents can discourage it. *Chatelaine*, 66(10): 36–7.

Mellor, A. (1991) Helping victims, in M. Elliott (ed.) *Bullying – a practical guide to coping for schools*. Harlow: Longman.

Mellor, A. (1995) *Which way now? A progress report on action against bullying in Scottish schools*. Edinburgh: Scottish Council for Research in Education.

Mooij, T. (1993) Working towards understanding and prevention in The Netherlands, in D. Tattum (ed.) *Understanding and Managing Bullying*. Oxford, Heinemann.

Morgan, G. (1986) *Images of Organisation*. London: Sage.

Mortimore, P., Sammons, P., Stoll, L., Lewis, D. and Ecob, R. (1988) *School Matters: the junior years*. Wells: Open Books.

Mulhern, S. (1994) *Preventing Youth Violence and Aggression*. Madison WI: State Department of Public Instruction.

Neary, A. and Joseph, S. (1994) Peer victimisation and its relationship to self-concept and depression among school girls. *Personality and Individual Differences*, 16(1): 183–86.

Newton, P. (1993) Malvern Girls College, in D. Tattum and G. Herbert (eds) *Countering bullying – Initiatives by schools and local authorities*. Stoke-on-Trent: Trentham Books.

Nolin, M. (1995) *Student Victimisation at School: Statistics in brief*. Washington DC: National Center for Educational Statistics.

O'Keefe, J.M (1994a) New leadership for a new initiative: presidents of public schools. *University Council for Educational Administration Conference, Philadelphia PA, October 1994*.

O'Keefe, M. (1994b) Linking marital violence, mother–child, father–child, aggression and child behaviour problems. *Journal of Family Violence*, 9: 1.

O'Moore, A.M. and Hillery, B. (1991) Bullying in Dublin schools. *Irish Journal of Psychology*, 10: 426–41.

Office for Standards in Education (OFSTED) (1995) *Guidance on the Inspection of Secondary Schools*. London: HMSO.

Olweus, D. (1978) *Aggression in the Schools: Bullies and whipping boys*. Washington DC: Hemisphere.

Olweus, D. (1983) Low school achievement and aggressive behaviour in adolescent boys, in N. Frude and H. Gault (eds) *Disruptive Behaviour in Schools*. New York: John Wiley.

Olweus, D. (1986) *Mobbning – Vad Ve Vet och Vad Vi Kan Göre. [Bullying – What We Know and What We Can Do]* Stockholm: Liber.

Olweus, D. (1989) Prevalence and incidence in the study of anti-social behaviour: definitions and measurement, in M. Klein (ed.) *Cross-National Research in Self-Reported Crime and Delinquency*. Dordrecht: Kluwer.

Olweus, D. (1991) Bully/victim problems among schoolchildren: basic facts and effects of a school-based intervention program, in D. Pepler and K. Rubin (eds) *The Development and Treatment of Childhood Aggression*. Hillsdale NJ: Erlbaum.

Olweus, D. (1993) *Bullying at School: What we know and what we can do*. Oxford: Blackwell.

Olweus, D. (1994) Bullying at school: basic facts and effects of school based intervention programme. *Journal of Child Psychology*, 35(7): 1171–90.

Payzant, T. (1992) New beginnings in San Diego: developing a strategy for interagency co-operation. *Phi Delta Kappan*, 3: 140.

Pearce, J. (1991) What can be done about the bully?, in M. Elliott (ed.) *Bullying – a practical guide to coping for schools*. Harlow: Longman.

Peplar, D.J., Craig, W., Ziegler, S. and Charach, A. (1994) An evaluation of anti-bullying intervention in Toronto schools. *Canadian Journal of Community Mental Health*, 13(2): 95–110.

Pervin, K. (1995) Parental attitudes and beliefs about bullying: an investigation into parents whose children attend an inner-city school. *Pastoral Care in Education* 13(3): 14–19.

Pervin, K. and Turner, A. (1994) An investigation into staff and pupils' knowledge, attitudes and beliefs about bullying in an inner city school. *Pastoral Care in Education*, 12(3): 16–22.

Pipho, C. (1994) Parental support for education. *Phi Delta Kappan*, 76(4): 270–2.

Pitts, J. and Smith, P. (1996) Preventing school bullying. *Police Research and Development Group Crime Detection and Prevention Paper 63*. London: Home Office.

Quicke, J. (1995) Positive bullying or pragmatic realism? Ways of seeing the self in pupil discourse. *Educational and Child Psychology* 12(3): 57–64.

Ramoutar, K. (1995) Social class and crime in a Caribbean community. *International Journal of the Sociology of Law* 23(3): 273–93.

Randall, P. (1996) *A Community Approach to Bullying*. Stoke-on-Trent: Trentham.

Reid, K., Hopkins, D. and Holly, P. (1987) *Towards the Effective School*. Oxford: Blackwell.

Roland, E. (1980) *Terror I Skolen*. Stavanger: Universitets Forlaget.

Roland, E. (1993) Bullying: a developing tradition of research and management, in D. Tattum (ed.) *Understanding and Managing Bullying*. Oxford: Heinemann.

Rutherford, B. and Billig, S.H. (1995) Parent, family and community involvement in the middle grades. *Phi Delta Kappan*, 77(1): 64–9.

Rutter, M., Maughan, B., Mortimore, P. and Ouston, J. (1979) *Fifteen Thousand Hours: Secondary schools and their effects of children*. London: Open Books.

Schwartz, D. (1993) Antecedents of aggression and peer victimisation. *Conference for Research in Child Development*, New Orleans, March 25–28, organized by Society for Research in Child Development.

Scottish Education Department (1989) *Talking about Schools*. Edinburgh: HMSO.

Shakeshaft, C. (1995) Peer harassment in schools. *Journal for a Just and Caring Education*, 1(1): 30–44.

Siann, G. (1994) Who gets bullied? The effect of school, gender and ethnic group. *Educational Research*, 36(2): 123–34.

Sisken, L.S. (1994) *Realms of Knowledge: Academic departments in secondary schools*. London: David Fulton.

Slee, P. (1995) Bullying in the playground: children's perceptions of their play environment. *Children's Environments Quarterly* 12(3): 320–27.

Smith, P.K. and Sharp, S. (1994) *School Bullying: Insights and perspectives*. London: Routledge.

Squires, D.A. and Kranyik, R.D. (1995) The Comer programme: changing school culture. *Educational Leadership* 53(4): 29–32.

Stanley, C. (1995) Teenage kicks: urban narratives of dissent not deviance. *Crime, Law and Social Change*, 23(2): 91–119.

Stein, N. (1995) Sexual harassment in school: the public performance of gendered violence. *Harvard Educational Review*, 65(2): 145–62.

Stoll, L. and Fink, D. (1996) *Changing our Schools*. Buckingham: Open University Press.

Stone, C.R. (1995) School community collaboration: comparing three initiatives. *Phi Delta Kappan* 76(10): 794–800.

Stott, K. and Walker, A. (1992) The nature and use of mission statements in Singaporean schools. *Educational Management and Administration* 20(1): 49–57.

Tattum, D. and Lane, D. (eds) (1989) *Bullying in Schools*. Stoke-on-Trent: Trentham Books.

Tattum, D. and Tattum, E. (1992) Bullying; a whole school response, in N. Jones and E. Baglin-Jones (eds) *Learning to Behave*. London: Kogan Page.

Tattum, D. and Herbert, G. (1993) *Countering Bullying – Initiatives by schools and local authorities*. Stoke-on-Trent: Trentham Books.

Tattum, D., Tattum, E. and Herbert, G. (1993) *Bullying in Secondary Schools*. Cardiff: Drake Educational Associates.

Thompson, D., Sharp, S., Ellis, M. and Rose, D. (1994a) *Improving Schools: establishing and integrating whole school behaviour*. London: David Fulton.

Thompson, D., Whitney, I. and Smith, P.K. (1994b) Bullying of children with special needs in mainstream schools. *Support for Learning* 19(3): 103–6.

Van Acker, R. (1995) A close look at school violence. *Update on Law-related Education*, 19(2): 4–8.

Van Reenan, L. (1992) Bullying in community and youth work. *Youth and Policy*, 38: 16–23.

Vriens, L.J. (1995) Coping with violence in schools: the challenge of limited possibilities. *Thresholds in Education*, 21(2): 18–25.

Wallace, M. (1991) Flexible planning: a key to the management of multiple innovations. *Educational Management and Administration*, 19(3): 180–93.

Weissglass, J. and Weissglass, T.L. (1987) *Learning, Feelings and Educational Change. Part one: Overcoming learning distress*. Santa Barbara CA: Kimberley Press.

West, A. and Varlaam, A. (1991) Choosing a secondary school: parents of junior school children. *Educational Research*, 33(1): 31–41.

Whitney, I. and Smith, P.K. (1993) A survey of the nature and extent of bully/victim problems in junior/middle and secondary schools. *Educational Research*, 35(1): 3–25.

Whitney, I., Rivers, I., Smith, P.K. and Sharp, S. (1994) The Sheffield project: methodology and findings, in P.K. Smith and S. Sharp (eds) *School Bullying: insights and perspectives*. London: Routledge.

Wilczenski, F. (1994) Practicing fair play: interventions for children as victims and victimisers. *Annual Meeting of National Association of School Psychologists, March 4–5, 1994, Seattle WA*.

Williams, D. and Schaller, K. (1993) Peer persuasion; a study of children's dominance strategies. *Early Child Development and Care*, 88: 31–41.

Young, G. (1994) Intervention Skills and a Willingness to Participate in Decreasing School Bullying. Doctoral Thesis, Nova University, Fort Lauderdale FL.

Ziegler, S. (1987) *The effects of parent involvement on children's achievement; the significance of home–school links*. Ontario: Toronto Board of Education.

Ziegler, S. and Rosenstein-Manner, M. (1991) *Bullying at school: Toronto in an international context (196R)*. Ontario: Toronto Board of Education.

# INDEX